High-Hee

High-Heeled Success
what it takes

marcia griffin

K
KERR

First published 1998
Kerr Publishing Pty Ltd
3 O'Connor Street
Chippendale NSW 2008
Australia
Telephone: Int +61 +2 +9699 5417
Facsimile: Int +61 +2 +96992065
ORDERS ONLY: http//www.ozemail.com.au\~pfa
OR pfa@ozemail.com.au

© Marcia Griffin 1998

This book is copyright. Apart from fair dealing for the purposes of private study, research, criticism or review, as permitted under the Copyright Act, no part may be reproduced by any process without written permission from Kerr Publishing Pty Ltd or the recording of copying by Copyright Agency Ltd under their rules for use

Cover design by Hall & Jones, Brisbane
Cover photography by Julian Kingma, Melbourne
Typeset in 11/13 Goudy Old Style by DOCUPRO, Sydney
Printed by Griffin Press, Adelaide

Distributed by TOWER BOOKS in Australia
Distributed by ADDENDA in New Zealand

National Library of Australia cataloguing-in-publication data:

Griffin, Marcia.
High-heeled success.

ISBN 1 875703 26 8.

1. Women in business—Australia. 2. Success in business—Australia. I. Title.

650.10820994

To the young businesswomen of Australia and New Zealand

may you achieve at the level you dream of,
have the financial independence you need,
and the happiness you seek

CONTENTS

Introduction   9

Book One
1 My Bad Attitude   15
2 OK, You've Sold Me   26
3 The Door   33

Book Two
4 Face Value   49
5 Home Life   55
6 Ticket to Ride   77
7 A Tough Call   86
8 The Buck Stops Here   91

Book Three

9	The Secrets of High-heeled Success	99
10	Dreams and Passion	103
11	The Best Laid Plans	107
12	Working Smart	117
13	Consistent Persistent Effort	124
14	Ssshhh!	131

Book Four

15	Women's Business	153
16	Lessons In Leadership	165
17	Selling Secrets	172
18	Japanese	181
19	Managing Money	190
20	Change	195

Recommended reading	201
Contacts	203
Acknowledgments	205

INTRODUCTION

*If you're not in business for fun or profit,
what are you
doing here?*

Robert Townsend, *Up The Organisation*

Business is about people. Business is about passion. Business is about fun. Business is about money. And the equation is simple: women excel in handling people; women are passionate; 'Girls Just Wanna Have Fun', as Cindy Lauper sang; and I can't think of a single woman who wouldn't know what to do with more money, though money itself isn't everything.

When management expert Robert Townsend wrote 'If you're not in business for fun or profit, what are you doing here?' 30 years ago, his audience was almost exclusively men—there were so few women senior enough in business to take on his ideas. It's better now, although it isn't good enough. Not even close.

I more or less founded a company and was its chief executive officer over 15 years of challenge, frustration, success, failures, mistakes, hard work and fun. It grew because I watered, nourished and protected it, and hired some of the finest saleswomen in Australia and New Zealand. Men had a role in the company's early days, one a vital one, but more than 95 per cent of the sweat was female and more than 95 per cent of the reward went to the same women. This has given me an insight into what holds women back—and I firmly believe this resides in the hearts and minds of women themselves.

One of my motives for writing this book is selfish. One of my favorite parts of the world is Aspen, Colorado, and I love skiing the powder there. I wish more women like me could—if the invitation appealed—at short notice take the time and devote the funds to come too. They'd need to be women with the money, flexible time and the sole deciding rights to do it. And there just aren't enough of them. But there is a wider purpose, too. Business is a tool—an unsurpassed tool—to get what you want by selling and giving to others. If I can help empower more women to meet their undeniably high potential in the business world then I will have met my goals with this book.

We are not like men—the saying, 'Men are from Detroit, women are from Paris' has a certain ring of truth to it—and the world of work is still, if not wholly a man's world any more, one largely designed for and operated by men using male rules, values and methods. As women we can do well to study why this is so.

And while impediments to women's progress still exist in the business world, these are much fewer than only a few years ago. It seems an inescapable conclu-

INTRODUCTION

sion: in many cases it is women who hold themselves back. Many women need to take an extra step, one men don't have to bother with. Men's desire for success seems to come naturally, something they have developed and passed on to each other over centuries. Women have to really *desire* success. Madly. Wildly. Deeply. Passionately. From there it is a matter of planning, goal setting, working the plan, not giving up and being positive. It can be hard work but the rewards are worth it: financial independence alone makes it so.

Business is essentially a tool to help us get what we want out of life. The obstacles on your path to success are not insurmountable.

Go for the top.

Marcia Griffin
Melbourne, 1998

Book One

A Quick (Embarrassing) Look Back

You are allowed to look back at the past,
but you are not allowed to stare.

Let your dreams take command,
not your regrets.

You never learn less.

1
MY BAD ATTITUDE

We cannot succeed by staying in our comfort zone
saying written in the front of my diary April 1982

I was broke, my marriage was on the rocks and I needed a job. Scanning the morning paper, an advertisement caught my eye:

SALES MANAGER — SOFT FURNISHINGS

That was up my street. I'd owned an upmarket gift-and-furnishing shop in the late 1970s and knew something about this. But what made me call was what came below the headline:

BEAUTIFUL OFFICES

Curiosity got me; I had to call.

The number on the ad was a personnel agency in the outer eastern Melbourne suburb of Glen Waverley. The woman who answered asked me to come for an interview. So, that afternoon, from the six-bedroom mansion in Toorak my husband and I were only a year from selling to pay our debts, I drove my Honda Accord along the main artery to the suburbs.

The personnel agency was in a pokey office up two flights of stairs in a suburban shopping centre. *These offices were far from beautiful.*

This doesn't look promising. What am I doing here?

My interview began with the woman telling me about the man who ran the soft-furnishing business.

'He's a wonderful man, a brilliant entrepreneur. His company is growing and soft furnishings are only one part of it.'

The sell got harder after I showed her my CV and talked about my background — two university degrees, three years as a teacher, an executive for the Wool Corporation, running my own import-retail business, working as a marketing consultant.

'You'll have to meet this man,' she said.

Sure, I said. But tell me more about his business. What does he do? Where does he work?

She dodged the questions and wouldn't tell me any more. I would have to meet him.

Never heard of him. This is a waste of time. Why did I come all the way out here to learn nothing? Is she hiding something? Maybe she knows nothing about the company. No job description. This is unprofessional. Perhaps there's something fishy going on . . .

I drove back to Toorak, feeling frustrated. I'd have to keep looking.

MY BAD ATTITUDE

Half an hour later, as I sat in the kitchen with a cup of tea, scanning the newspaper, the phone rang.

'Hello, let me introduce myself. My name's John Taylor. You spoke to the personnel company this morning about a job. I've just been told about you and I'd like to meet you. Are you free this afternoon?'

This was better. I still wanted to see those offices so I said yes.

I took the same route east from Toorak, this time ending up in an industrial area of Mulgrave, in a street of warehouses and factories.

From the outside John Taylor's offices looked good. The building was brick, two storeys and well maintained. It had a 1970s feel, with orange paint and brown exposed bricks. The shock was inside.

After being shown through reception I walked into the biggest office I'd ever seen. It was huge.

The office of the general manager of the Wool Corporation could be dropped in here as a broom cupboard. At the corporation the size of your office depended on seniority. This man was just pleasing himself.

In one corner was a semi-circular desk. Behind the desk stood a brown leather chair. On my side of the desk were several upholstered brown chairs.

Sitting behind the desk as I walked in was a man pushing 40, resplendent in a bright red shirt, open to the waist almost, a big thick gold chain and chest hair poking out. Huge room, huge desk, huge chair.

And oh my God, red shirt, gold chain, chest hair.

I was wearing one of my best business suits, all of

which came from an exclusive Collins Street store where I bought all my clothes. This one was dark blue, Italian and made from top-quality wool. With beautiful leather shoes and light make-up, I was impeccably groomed. And I was just fascinated by the way this man looked. No tie, no suit; he was just pleasing himself.

He's just wrong. People in corporate life just don't look like this.

But I was still impressed by the size of his office. It was extraordinary. It was so big. The advertisement wasn't wrong.

I held out my hand. He grabbed it.

'Mr Taylor.'

'G'day. Call me John. Take a seat, Marcia.'

I sat in one of the brown chairs. He leaned forward and picked up my CV, which had been passed on by the personnel company. It was beautifully set out — I'd spent hours tracing my life and career since my first day at school. I'd posed for a professional photographer and the resulting color photograph was stapled in the top corner. He flicked through it, half interested. 'Oh yeah,' he said aloud to himself.

I can't believe this. He's treating my university degrees like they're primary-school report cards! (I now see I was part-way to becoming an educated derelict, but that was then.)

'Let's see. You're married, you're livin' in Toorak. You went to private school, university. Then you did some teachin'?'

'That's right. I taught in high schools for three years. Mostly French, English, history.'

'And then you went travellin' overseas for a year?'

'That's right.'

My God! His English is dreadful. There are no g-s on the end of words. I can't work for someone like this. I've been to private school, I've done elocution lessons, I've got university degrees, I've done an English major . . .

'An' you got a job at the Wool Corporation. Research economist. So what does that mean? What did you do there?'

'Well, I studied overseas markets to determine the future price of wool. My reports helped the board set the reserve price for wool. The board needed to know fashion trends, competitive fibre trends, industry trends and so on, so I travelled often to Europe and met manufacturers to research the issues. Mostly Italy, France, Britain and Germany.'

'Sounds a good job. Why d'ya leave?'

'I'd had enough of corporate life. Being a woman I felt my opportunities to climb the ladder were limited. So I started my own business.'

'That's this shop? Pocomella?'

'Yes, in High Street, Armadale. I set it up with my partner and ran it for two years. It was a great success.'

'I know the shop. I went into it a few times. It was such a pretty shop.'

I beamed.

I don't remember him as a customer. But my shop had

some beautiful goods. Perhaps he has got good taste, after all . . .

'Yeah, I went into your shop and I knocked off your ideas.'

What?!

'You had those beautiful English fabrics and cushions. They were too expensive, so I got someone to copy them. At a factory in Moorabbin. And I sell 'em for a fraction of the price you did.'

He's selling copies of my cushions. Making thousands of dollars. How dare he come into my shop and steal my ideas!

I was a bit stunned by this.
'What sort of business is this?'
'It's diverse. We sell pottery and soft furnishings all around the country.'
'How did you get into it?'
'I was lucky I guess. I left school at 15. My parents couldn't afford the train fare for me. So I went to work, eventually gettin' an apprenticeship as a plumber. I ended up my plumbing career as a marketing manager, then I got out and went searchin' for my own business. After travellin' around Australia I came across this pottery in Ballarat. I started sellin' jugs, cups, bowls — the lot — to friends and neighbors from the boot of my car. Did a few markets, too. Then I got others to sell it. And today I've got a thousand women sellin' pottery around Australia. And soft furnishings, too. Like the ones from your shop.'

'But what do you do?'

'I direct-sell the product.'

'I'm sorry. I don't understand what that means.'

'Well, our sales team make appointments to go into their friends' homes, and show the goods to that person and their friends. Some people call it party plan. Have you heard of it?'

Party Plan! Euughh! Terrible stuff. What a nightmare — those sort of women. Who does he think I am?

'But let me show you what we do here. Come downstairs to the warehouse.'

He led me out of his huge office down a flight of stairs to an even bigger room that was a showroom for the company's pottery. It turned out consultants could come here and choose what they wanted to take on their sales trips.

This stuff is horrible. It's brown and ugly. How could anyone buy this?

'Sells like hot cakes, this product. I turned over $6 million last year.'

How much?!

'And the soft furnishings are kicking on well. Here, have a look at these.'

He pointed to another display room packed with cushions, bedspreads and fabrics. It looked very familiar. I pulled the closest cushion within an inch of my nose and inspected the fabric.

Look at the stitching. And it's made of poor quality cotton. Cheap imitation. Just as I thought.

I looked at the range of designs. Many were based on the exclusive Designer Guild fabrics I'd imported.

They've changed the pattern just enough to avoid legal problems. The cheek of this man. Stealing my cushions, then boasting about it.

I looked about and my eye caught more brown pots.

Yuk!

'I'm sorry. I just can't sell these products.'
'Yeah, no worries. Let's go back to the office.'
He smiled, a bit indulgently, I thought. I will not be condescended to, but he was polite. No wonder. When I ran my shop my accountant was very impressed at our first year's turnover of $150,000 — we even made a small profit. Yet here was a business built from scratch that was turning over millions.

But my decision on his stock stood. The elite, upmarket items at my Armadale shop had been a great deal better.

Who would I know who'd want to buy a cheap copy of what I'd been selling in my shop? No. I can't see it. It won't work.

The advertisement said SALES MANAGER and I had figured out that I'd be my own manager; a saleswoman. Party plan. Selling to people I knew.

No. Couldn't work. Wouldn't work.

MY BAD ATTITUDE

John Taylor led me back to his office to continue our talk.

Were all the years I'd spent at university wasted? I live in Toorak. We've got a house in Portsea. I'm intelligent, educated. I deserve a proper career, a proper job, a good life, not . . . this!

The huge office overwhelmed me again.

He left school at 15 and he's offering me a job. What's gone wrong here?

I sat back in the chair as he continued talking about his company. Since I'd first walked into this huge office with the curved desk, something had been nagging away at me. Suddenly it hit me:

I'm sitting on the wrong side of the desk. He should be asking me for a job. It's all the wrong way round.

'Excuse me,' I said, interrupting his flow.
'I think there's something wrong here. I can't work out why I'm sitting on this side of the desk and you're on that side.'

His arm dropped to the desk and he looked squarely at me, full gold chain on a hairy mat, framed by a red shirt. He was taken aback for a moment, but not for long.

'I think I know.'
Silence followed.

Come on Marcia, you're broke, your marriage is over, you need some runs on the board. You haven't got many options. Find out! Ask him! You don't want to go back to corporate life, you haven't any money to set up a business. Ask him!

'Tell me.'
'Attitude.'

What do you mean by attitude? My attitude's fine.

'You need to understand attitude and what it means.'

'?'

'And you can start by the way you're speaking. The way you see yourself. The way you see the world around you. The way you see other people. But most of all you've got an attitude that selling is beneath you.'

My body language went defensive. 'Well, I just can't see myself in sales.'

I've been a shop owner — and in marketing — but not sales. I'm not in sales.

'Well, Marcia, you can't see yourself in the business world if that's the case because every business is about selling. Every business is about communicating with your customer. And if you can't see yourself in sales you're probably never going to make it in life.'

Not long afterwards our talk ended with nothing said about a specific job.

He said, 'There's something else I want to talk to you about. Come back another day; we'll make another time.'

He was giving me a bit of time to adjust. He kept talking about his turnover, how many people he had in the team.

MY BAD ATTITUDE

I left intrigued and fascinated. This man who spoke such poor English, who dressed the way he dressed, was in the largest office I'd ever been in. And he was on to something, but I didn't know what it was.

It was food for thought as I drove back to Toorak.

2
OK, YOU'VE SOLD ME

Courage = commitment + doubt + action

written in my diary

Two days later, John Taylor phoned again.

'I'd really like to talk to you again about this. I feel you should look at it very seriously.'

'I don't think it is me. I can't see myself selling your soft furnishings. Or pottery.'

But I remembered his words: 'You think selling's beneath you. It's your attitude.'

He talked for several minutes and said there were other opportunities, beyond cushions and pots.

So I decided to talk to him again. I was curious.

How did direct selling really work? What did the man know that I didn't?

OK, YOU'VE SOLD ME

A day later I was back in the huge office on the wrong side of the big desk.

We talked further about selling — ideas mostly — and he explained the advantages of direct selling. Little investment, no overheads, no geographical limitations — and having run a shop those advantages were clear enough.

I didn't have to buy tons of stock, pay rent and wasn't stuck in one street. Until that moment I'd seen retail as the only way of selling — where the customers come to you. Here, the goods went to the customer. And most important, it worked. Why else would 1000 people be making money for themselves and John Taylor? With the right product, this could work. And work for me.

John Taylor leaned behind his desk, reached into a cardboard box and pulled out several plastic packages. He put them on the desk. Each had Japanese characters on the labels.

'Here's some skin care samples. I'd like you to take them home, try them and tell me if you think they're any good.'

I picked one of the packages up, a foundation cream. In black roman letters was written the word:

Pola

I've never heard of them. And if I don't know them, they can't be important.

'OK, I'll try them.'

I'm sure they're rubbish, and when they turn out to be useless I'll happily tell this odd man what I think. And I'll be able to forget him and his downmarket products and silly marketing methods.

He beamed. The interview was over. I walked back to my car clutching a plastic bag of Pola products.

Six days later I was back in the big office. The samples I'd taken home proved fantastic; they felt quite special, better than the high-quality retail products I'd been using. I was amazed. I'd buy Estée Lauder, Christian Dior, but, wow, this Pola range was pretty amazing. I had desperately wanted to find the products horrible. Because intellectually that would let me off the hook. And I could forget about this man with his Mercedes and huge office and go back into corporate life.

But they weren't. They were great.

He explained he'd acquired the rights to distribute Pola products in Australia and New Zealand while vice-chairman of the Direct Selling Association. Pola, then a $US2 billion-a-year company, wanted to expand south and, being a member of the international association, got in touch with the national body. And John Taylor snared the deal as the franchisee for Japan's most successful direct-selling cosmetics company. But this didn't help my attitude. Nor did John Taylor when he looked directly at me and said 'You know, I think you're a cosmetics person.'

Hah! Rubbish. He doesn't know my husband buys my make-up and had since we married. First stolen cushions, then horrible pottery. Now painted faces.

My image of cosmetics was none too positive. Like most people I'd seen the painted dolls on the ground

OK, YOU'VE SOLD ME

floor of department stores wearing white coats, wearing too much make-up and putting tester products on women.

Yet the more John Taylor told me about Pola the more genuinely interested I became. He produced a dozen different products from the Pola ranges — toners, cleansers, moisturisers, lipsticks and mascaras — arranging them in a neat row on his desk. There were some booklets, with pictures. All the writing was in Japanese. The parent company spent more than $150 million each year on research. It was involved in genetic engineering, medical research, exploring ancient Chinese remedies and herbs. And in Japan, a nation of discerning consumers, it was a household name. About 150,000 women — the Pola ladies — sold the product. Five million women used it. This was direct-selling Japanese style.

Then he started to talk about the size of the cosmetic market in Australia; hundreds of millions of dollars.

'Do you know any women who don't use cosmetics or skin care?'

'No. I can't think of one.'

'What about your bathroom?'

'I've got a cupboard full.'

'So how much do you spend on cosmetics each year?'

I had no idea.

It was something I just did. Almost a necessity. But probably hundreds of dollars. I didn't really know.

He told me the industry was worth nearly $1 billion

a year — and skin care products were the most lucrative area.

'And skin care is what Pola does best.'

Wow. This is a big business. But how come I've never heard of Pola?

But I really loved using them and, no matter how hard I tried, I couldn't ignore the fact that I liked them better than the Estée Lauder and Christian Dior that my husband Neil had bought for me. The moisturiser was the clincher. It felt so much better going on to the skin. And within days I could see that my skin looked better. The effect was even greater a few weeks down the track.

My delight as a consumer began to change my attitude.

It was time to bring my seven years as a research economist into play. Over the next few days I tried more of the samples — all proved excellent.

I visited the Japanese consulate and asked if they had heard of Pola. Certainly they had — it was a Japanese institution — and they spoke of it in glowing terms.

I contacted the Australian Bureau of Statistics to get research on the cosmetics industry. There was no specific data, but it was clear it was a huge industry.

One figure I came across was telling: men spend 18 per cent of their income on their personal appearance; women spend 31 per cent.

I called the Direct Selling Association to find out more about John Taylor's company. Even though it looked great — the pottery, soft furnishings and cosmetics — and he seemed to be making lots of money, I had no context to put it in. They gave him the thumbs up — he was an established and respected player.

Finally I phoned a friend who had a big cosmetic manufacturing business in Melbourne's western suburbs. His family had been in this business for a long time: he would be the key.

Had he heard of Pola?

Yes. And he'd even been to Japan to look at their facilities — this was one of the most impressive skin care companies in the world. Their research was extraordinary, he said. If you have an opportunity to be associated with the product go ahead, he advised me.

A few days later I was back in the big office.

At John Taylor's suggestion, I went out with one of the consultants from the pottery division to watch a sale in someone's home.

I left stunned.

There were only four 'customers', the 'pottery consultant' and a huge amount of pottery on display — and sales were more than $500. I was intrigued. At 25 per cent, the saleswoman was making $125 for an hour or so of work. And this was in 1982 dollars.

If they can sell that much dark brown, ugly pottery, imagine what I could do with cosmetics of high quality.

I could see the value of taking the product into the home. It wasn't being left on the shelf — it was being taken to the customer's home, where they were often more relaxed and open to ideas.

I could see how referral business worked. Going into the home generated new work, word-of-mouth advertising the business.

But could I do this?

3
THE DOOR

*Success comes from doing the things
other people aren't prepared to do*

written in my diary

Two weeks after my first meeting with John Taylor, I made the decision to go ahead and sell cosmetics.

My God, what are you doing? Are you mad? Why, Marcia, why?

In part, I needed a challenge: my marriage was collapsing and I wanted to plunge into something. This was unknown territory, exciting as well as scary.

But what clinched it was the Pola story. The company was top-class in its research, products and quality. I'd tried their products and I knew they were good. It was something I believed in, something I could sell to my friends.

Test marketing on people in John Taylor's company

had been very positive. But was this enough to start a business?

How would I know until I tried?

In my first weeks John Taylor provided essential guidance — without it, I know I would have quit.

His sayings kept me going, gave me the strength to battle on. The most memorable: 'Successful people do the things that unsuccessful people aren't prepared to do.'

Another: 'Be careful who you get advice from. Only listen to people who are more successful than yourself.'

But most important, he prepared me for the fact that people would sow seeds of doubt in my mind.

'Marcia, people will tell you you're wrong. You're foolish. You're making the wrong decision.'

'I know. Sometimes I think it is the wrong decision.'

'Why?'

'I think people will laugh at me, think I'm stupid. That's my big fear.'

'Well, you may feel really hesitant about what you're doing but you can't ever show it. The key to success in life and business and negotiation is that you never show any fear.'

'How do I do that?'

'Well, whatever comes along over the next few weeks you're going to have lots of rejection, lots of people laughing at you, but you've got to always let them feel that you are in control. Don't let someone else's doubts affect your decision.'

THE DOOR

And he was right about the unwanted advice. My first steps were buffeted by people's reactions and I soon learned a great deal more about attitude, especially negative attitude and how to deal with it. Over the weeks and months to come, friends told me I was wrong, foolish, mistaken. All the things I'd already thought.

Even my husband Neil had doubts. He wasn't negative, he was just unsure. I think he didn't understand. He didn't discourage me, but didn't encourage me either. I guess it was a sign that communication was deteriorating in our marriage. Perhaps he thought I'd gone off the rails — I sometimes thought the same.

Yet having made the decision to be the first person to sell these unknown Japanese cosmetics, the next step was to get on the telephone to my friends, make appointments and convince them to buy the goods.

This was the hardest part.

But having made the decision to get started, I had to do it.

I drew up a list of all the women I knew and, in the months that followed, I kept this list at my side. It grew all the time, becoming pages long, as names were added, others crossed out with notes next to them. Each time I thought of new people I added them to the list. It was a mix of personal friends, people I'd worked with, people I'd mixed with — a broad list.

I sat for a long time going through the list.

Who would I call first? Who should I avoid?

The thought of getting on the phone and making

contact with my friends, trying to sell them cosmetics, had been holding me back.

It amazed me the network I'd built up that had gone untapped as I realised I knew dozens and dozens of people. I could have kicked myself for not having kept a proper list of my customers at my shop in Armadale — they'd bought high-quality fabrics and would have been ideal candidates for Pola lines, which don't have cheap price-tags.

This was an early lesson on how important a good database is.

Of course it was one thing to draw up my list — it was another to pick up the phone.

I need a soft listener, someone who won't challenge me. Now let's see: ah! Mary-Ellen.

I'd met Mary-Ellen in the mid-1970s; we were neighbors and both newlyweds. Her enthusiasm was infectious and she had been a great supporter over the years.

I had to start somewhere positive. On my list, she was the best bet.

Pick up that phone, Marcia. Successful people . . .

'Mary-Ellen. Hi. It's Marcia. How are you?'
'Oh, I'm great. How are you.'
'Fantastic, Mary-Ellen. I haven't spoke to you for a few weeks, but apart from ringing to say hello . . .

Deep breath, Marcia. Here goes.

. . . the other reason I'm calling is because I've decided to go into this new business and I'm really excited about it. I've come across a range of Japanese skin care and cosmetic products that I'd never heard of before, and I've been using them for a few weeks and I'm really impressed with the results. And I'd love to show them to you.'

'Right.'

'But before I do that I'd like to tell you a little bit about the company, because perhaps you think this is a little strange for me to be doing this considering my past. I came across this product because I met the man with the franchise and it turns out this company is one of the largest cosmetic and skin care companies in the world. And it sells its products on a direct selling basis. So we're not going to be putting this product in department stores or pharmacies, we're going to be selling it in people's houses. And I have to say to you Mary-Ellen, I don't know a lot about direct selling except that it's very successful. And now I've done some research on the direct selling industry I know it's a great way to show someone a product. And I would love to come and show you this product. It's just so impressive. What we'll be doing is I'll come along, give you a facial, let you try the products and if you can invite some of your friends who you know are interested in skin care and cosmetics, that would be great. Does this sound interesting to you?'

Please, please, please say 'Yes'.

'Yes, I'd love to do that because I have problems with my skin. I've got sensitive skin.'

Yes, yes, yes.

'I know that, that's one of the reasons I called you. But I'm also calling you because the product is so good and I want you to be one of the first people in Melbourne to see it.'

'I'd love to do it. What exactly do you want me to do?'

'Well, if you invite six or eight people I'll give you a facial and explain why the product's so good and how to use it — because I don't think most women know how to use skin care products and cosmetics — and that's all we need to do. If we make it about 7.30 in the evening, if that's OK with you, and I'll be there about 7.15 to set the products up and sort things out. Just ask some of the girls you know who are interested in skin care and their appearance. So let's work out a date.'

She was very open and we set a date for two weeks' time. It could have been sooner but I was far from ready. I had little idea what to do at a presentation. This wasn't pottery, it was cosmetics. And I was supposed to know all about it!

My *first appointment. Help!*

Mary-Ellen's enthusiasm and willingness turned out to be the exception rather than the rule. John Taylor was right. Once I picked up the phone and began calling I ran into a wave of negative attitudes.

Susie, for example, was someone I regarded as a good friend, someone in my Toorak social network who I'd known a long time. And I knew she was interested in skin care.

She's sure to be a supporter.

    I rang.
    'Hello Susie, it's Marcia here. How are you?'
    'Fine.'
    'I'm ringing not only to say hello . . . '

Here goes . . .

    And as my sales pitch went on I could hear her hesitancy.
    She was absolutely charming, but I could hear 'Oh God, I don't want to have to see this stuff.'
    And I knew she used a product called Erno Laszlo, an exclusive expensive product you could only buy from a magnificent counter in Georges. It was very upmarket. My cardboard box of products was going to struggle to compete with this.
    She was very sceptical. 'Japanese?'
    So I had to explain there are 1000 companies making skin care products in Japan.
    'Have you heard of Shiseido?'
    'Yes.'
    But she didn't see it on the same level as Erno Laszlo.

This is tough. A big effort . . .

    'Pola, of course, is much above Shiseido . . .'
    But I could hear her hesitancy and knew I was not going to convince her to even look at the product.
    'Just try it Susie, just have a look at it.'
    But she wouldn't.
    'Marce, I'm absolutely happy with Erno Laszlo.'

She had a complete prejudice.

What's wrong with you, Susie? I thought you had an open mind . . .

And there was another person, not a close friend but someone I had a fair bit of contact with. I'll call her Jane.

I called, and began my sales patter. She interrupted: 'Oh, this sounds like complete rubbish. I can't believe you're doing this.'

And she basically hung up on me.

I saw Jane about 14 years later — in mid-1996 — and she came up to me at a party and said, 'Your success is so incredible. I must have a look at your product some time.'

For some people, Jane included, success is everything. She never tried any Pola products though.

My great list often was turned on its head. Those I thought would support me were negative. Those who I doubted turned out to be fantastic.

This was most surprising among my close friends, some of whom were extraordinarily negative. They didn't even want to try the product and suggested I call other people. They were nervous, hesitant.

John Taylor had forewarned me about this.

'Remember two rules,' he said. 'Don't rely on your friends and don't believe what they say about business, unless they are successsful business people themselves.'

He told me not to ask any of my close friends what

they thought about my selling Pola. There was wisdom behind this. Some were surprised, some shocked and, had I listened to their advice, I may well have ended my Pola career in 1982. He told me that when you ask the wrong people, your whole life can be affected.

'In business, seek advice from people who know about business,' he added. Because it's important to differentiate between friendship and business. And sometimes that's hard to do.

It was hard not to take rejections personally because it was as if I was saying, 'This is a good product, you should see it, let me show you.' And when they put me off with a weak excuse, I took it as a personal rejection, because it was my personal recommendation. But I had to remember I wasn't suggesting a film or play or restaurant. I was trying to sell something.

Next to each name on my list I put the person's response — and there were more negatives than positives.

The negatives, for example:

- I'm unwell
- Get back to me later
- Please send me some literature
- I don't know about that
- I'm happy with my brand
- Phone back in June
- You're not a beautician — what do you know about this?

The positives:
- Yes, send some samples
- I may know someone interested in joining the company
- Yes, I'll have a presentation
- I'll let friends know and call back.

I remember the feeling of rejection as people said, 'No' or 'Call back'. But I had made a commitment to myself to get results, to keep taking the rejections. I told myself it was part of the process, I had to keep going. But despite attempts to remain positive, my negative thoughts were strong.

Really, Marcia. This wasn't such a good idea. It wasn't going to work anyway. Who do you think you are that you can start a new brand on the Australian market?

Giving up would have been easy. It was a battle to stay positive, to remember what John Taylor had told me.

This product is great. Believe in what you are doing.

I kept this thought in my mind until I spoke to people who were interested.

Every time I picked up the phone I had to think positively, gear myself for rejection — and not show surprise when finally someone said, 'Yes, I'll have a look at it.' And sometimes it took a lot of powerful persuasion to get people interested.

All I did for the first few weeks was get on the phone. It's different today — the Pola sales team can give away free samples and win people's interest that way. They also have a big company structure behind them. It's a little easier.

John Taylor reinforced my 'attitude' several times in the first weeks. He talked about overcoming these obstacles, keeping going, not being daunted by negativity and understanding negativity is someone's fear of change, of trying something new — not a personal rejection of me.

Of course every woman I knew was already using some brand. The market was thick with products, some heavily advertised. The image of Estée Lauder, for example, was deeply entrenched in the minds of everyone I contacted. It wasn't as if they'd been waiting all their lives for Pola.

What terrified me though was going into someone's home and demonstrating the product. I'd put off Mary-Ellen's appointment for two weeks, but it grew steadily closer.

I had no idea about a proper skin care routine. I just did the basic things I'd been told by someone in a department store. I had no in-depth knowledge about skin care or cosmetics application. I just put it on.

I knew I needed to know more — then I realised my friends probably knew about as much as I did. They used cosmetics and skin care, but didn't spend time talking about these things. They weren't experts. So my approach of being fairly casual about the products was probably more appropriate than being serious.

My training was simple at best — the few notes from Pola I couldn't understand because they were in Japanese. There was no manual. So the only practical lesson came from John Taylor's teenage daughter, who gave me a complete facial — she knew more about the products than anyone else. She also gave me a facial massage, one step in the Pola procedure.

Later, at home, I tried the procedure on myself and got the order wrong. I had to keep looking at my checklist.

Are you sure you know what you are doing?

Inevitably, the evening of my first appointment — and I'll never forget the night of 7 June 1982 — my moment of truth, arrived. I had no idea how I'd go.

I was so nervous I went to the fridge at Toorak and took out a bottle of chardonnay. I opened it, poured a glass and wolfed it down. A second glass followed.

Well, cheers to the new career. Or my insanity! God, I'm nervous.

I was drinking alone. Neil was at his law office in Melbourne's Owen-Dixon chambers, where he worked till late most nights. He thought I'd lost it. He wasn't quite sure what was going on.

The drinks began to ease the speed with which questions had been running round my head.

Why am I doing this? Have I gone crazy? Why wasn't I just driving back from the city to prepare dinner for my husband, as I had done in my previous corporate life? Oh oh, time to go.

I walked out to my blue Honda, parked in the garage. Next door was a space where my husband parked his red Ferarri. He had a red Ferarri and I had a blue Honda — which was probably a telling story

THE DOOR

when I look back. We had drifted apart and were on very different journeys. Neil just didn't understand what I was doing.

I had a cardboard box with the products in it. Each had English writing on it but I knew I had to line them up to remind myself how to use them. I put the box in the car.

I was wearing a blue business suit, looking smart — and set off south along Orrong Road, a leafy street of big houses, a wealthy neighborhood, much like the one I was leaving behind in more ways than one. I drove south, before joining the Nepean Highway on the 20-minute trip to Mary-Ellen's house.

On the passenger seat was a box of Pola goodies — 30 or 40 products in bottles and tubes, with samples of creams, cleansers, masks, lotions and lipsticks. There were brochures that had been made for the US market but they were appalling, so I took only one, just for my reference.

So there were no sales aids. Through my mind went the theme John Taylor had drummed into my head.

Sell yourself, sell the company, sell the product. In that order.

On the floor of the car was my briefcase containing order forms, a calculator and pencils. For orders. Hopefully.

I pulled up outside her home in Menzies Street, Brighton. A big house, wealthy area. This was it. Trembling, I took out the box, put it on the bonnet, took the briefcase and, with the box under my arm, I walked up the gravel driveway to the front door, past the tennis court on the right hand side.

This is not such a good look. Better get something better than this cardboard box. Help!

I'd been to this house dozens of times before, but it was nothing like this.

Can I do it?

I walked, one foot in front of the other, stopped at the front door and knocked. Had someone told me then that this would be the start of a multi-million-dollar business and a 15-year success story, I would have laughed out loud and told them they were joking.

Life can be funny like that.

Book Two

My Business Journey

The only people with time to rock the boat
are those who aren't rowing

The most valuable thing you can give
anyone is your time

Business is a problem-solving exercise

4
FACE VALUE

'Would you tell me, please, which way I ought to go from here?' said Alice.
'That depends a good deal on where you want to get to,' said the Cat.

Lewis Carroll, *Alice in Wonderland*

Two months after presenting Mary-Ellen's friends with my range I found myself standing on stage in Tokyo in front of 3000 cheering Japanese. I could barely believe it.

Here I was, a woman with a collapsing marriage and only eight weeks' experience with cosmetics, standing next to a badly-dressed man who had left school at 15. And we were bring treated like heroes.

A big sign said,

WELCOME TO THE POLA CONVENTION
1982

The contrast to the warehouse in Mulgrave, to John Taylor's office, to the briefcase of samples I carried as the sole company representative — I stood blinking, amazed. John Taylor and I looked down at thousands of beaming faces, the only white people in a huge auditorium. The announcement of our names as part of Pola's new Australian division had brought cheers, shouts and enthusiastic applause. Some people shook rattles, others waved flags. Colored lights flashed, representing different sales teams. As we walked on stage some in the crowd gently threw mandarins at us (a sign of good luck, I was told).

If I'd had any doubts about how serious Pola was, they were quickly erased. On the first two days in Tokyo, John Taylor and I were shown the company's facilities. I couldn't have been more impressed.

The company was founded in 1929 by Shinobu Suzuki and named, rather oddly, after Pola Negri, a glamorous Polish-born silent film star who had an affair with Hollywood heartthrob Rudolph Valentino in the year before his death in 1926. Direct selling of cosmetics was the business from day one, with a chemicals division added in 1940. In 1954, Shinobu's son, Tsuneshi, took over, expanding the business into the United States and Asia. The company profile lists 1982 as the year it established its business in Australia.

We visited the research laboratories where the company spends more than $US150 million each year on medical and skin-care research, especially looking for cures to skin diseases. It also has a key joint-venture project with China, examining and extracting chemicals from traditional Chinese medicines. It employs 2000 people — including more than 200 chemists — and is at the cutting edge of some Japanese medical research. And it makes money — lots of it — by selling and developing cosmetics, perfumes, jewellery and lingerie.

In Japan, the company is an institution, the country's third biggest cosmetics firm. About 150,000 women are trained to sell the cosmetics and Pola ladies are as common in Japan as Avon ladies in America — except, perhaps, a Pola lady has a much higher status.

Japan's 150,000 women compared with one in Australia — me.

And on the evening of the conference, Taylor and I were taken to dinner by Pola's president Tsuneshi Suzuki and his interpreter. Tsuneshi Suzuki is married with no children, immensely rich, and has indulged himself in art — he has a world-renowned collection. The foyer of the Pola headquarters in Tokyo holds millions of dollars worth of statues by artists such as Renoir and Henry Moore. At dinner, we sat in a private room in one of Tokyo's top restaurants. On the table was a Japanese and an Australian flag. The food was exquisite; I have not eaten a better meal.

I remember little of the specific conversation, except that Mr Suzuki wished us good fortune and a long working partnership. For John Taylor, the partnership lasted five more years. But for me it was the next decade and a half.

The trip had been a reward for meeting sales quotas. But the quota had been quite modest and really it was a chance for John Taylor to show me the company and win me over. It worked.

I was like Alice at the crossroads. And once I'd seen what was in Tokyo, I knew which way I wanted to go.

And slowly, the Australian business grew: from one woman to two, three, four, 30 by the end of 1982 until, by the end of 1997, there were 4700 consultants in Australia and New Zealand. From a small loss we began to make serious money. In several years, we were the fastest growing division of Pola worldwide; even during the recession of the early 1990s, as companies across Australia folded, our business grew rapidly. Even the strengthening Japanese currency failed to stem growth: the product cost more, our margins were cut, but still the business expanded.

It began eight weeks before I met Mr Suzuki, half a world away, when I walked through Mary-Ellen's front door in Brighton. That was the first of hundreds of thousands of presentations in Australia, an evening that was a success for one reason. I sold $340 of product.

I was delighted, especially as I almost ran off when her front door opened. Instead of Mary-Ellen's smiling face I was met by her husband, a powerhouse in the Melbourne marketing world.

'Hello, Marcia, welcome. Look, Mary-Ellen's told me what you're up to and I'm curious. Would you mind if I sat in and watched you?'

This was the last thing I needed. I was nervous enough as it was.

But I smiled confidently.

'That's absolutely fine. I'd be delighted if you sit in.'

This was a trick John Taylor taught me. Put simply, he said: 'You are going to be really hesitant about what you are doing, but don't show it. You have to fake it till you make it.'

The simple truth, said Taylor, was that people mirror our behavior. So even when you're really nervous, you can't show it. Because if we are hesitant and nervous with people, they'll respond the same way. So I had to put on a brave front and told Mary-Ellen's husband to sit in.

The presentation was typical of thousands I did over the following years. There were six women (and Mary-Ellen's husband) in the dining room and I introduced myself and told them a little about Pola and about what I would be doing.

Before the presentation we all had a glass of wine, but during the demonstration I made sure there was no food or drink. I wanted people to concentrate on the product, and I also wanted to stop the evening from degenerating into a party. This was business and there was plenty of time for a glass of wine afterwards. And in most cases this was what happened.

'What I am going to show you is what you should do to yourself every morning and every evening,' I explained.

Then I took them through the process, using various Pola products on the hostess, Mary-Ellen: how to use a cleanser, a toner, massage the face, apply a mask, use moisturiser, foundation etc. My favorite line in my sales patter was — and still is — less is best. When it comes to presentation, I still dislike the painted faces that come from too much make-up.

That first Pola presentation is so clear in my memory, standing there in front of those women explaining what the Pola company was about, explaining why the product was so good and feeling as nervous as could be, knotted up inside, yet somehow carrying the night off. It was the first time I'd applied cosmetics to another person's face, and in doing the facial I forgot to use one of the key products. But no one seemed to notice.

And I not only sold $340 of product, I got two appointments for further presentations. It fascinated me that anyone wanted to go through this again. And I must say we had a lot of fun once I relaxed a bit but I was terribly nervous and tense at the start. But anyway, that was the start of the business and I can remember driving home that night thinking, 'If you can build a business, and you have a lot of people doing that, you could build a very big business.' But to me at that stage, it was a question of going out and doing it on my own.

I knew then where I was going. What was curious was that it had taken me so long to find out.

5

HOME LIFE

*Thoughts become words, words become action,
action habits, habits values, values destiny*

written in my diary

The Jesuits have a saying: 'Give me a child to the age of seven and I will give you the man.'

I believe this claim to a great extent because I realise the influence of my parents on me today: before I went to school I was taught to spell, read and count by my father. He had a great passion and faith in education, and encouraged me wherever possible. I spent little time with other children and learned to be independent. And my father instilled in me a simple saying: 'Do your best.' Upbringing doesn't absolutely make us, but it provides the platform for what we make of ourselves.

My parents had met at a country dance in rural Victoria. He was a farmer's son, she a farmer's daughter, the local primary school teacher. Both came from big

Catholic families that arrived in Australia in the 1860s, settling in the wide plains of western Victoria, where land was open for all comers.

My great uncle sold them a cheap property, and I was born not long after. My parents battled to make the farm pay in their first years of marriage, before we moved to a lusher farm in Victoria's Western District — they still live there.

I was the first of seven children. Being first you get plenty of attention early on; you're also the leader, whether you like it or not.

I thrived at primary school, but the competition was not keen. Wickliffe State School, Number 948, was tiny — in its biggest year it had 22 students. The classes ranged from prep to grade six, so small children were in the same classroom as boys and girls aged up to 13.

When I began, aged four, I had to sit in the row of desks closest to the door. The goal was to get to the row of desks by the window, because that was where grade six sat. They were the people with power, those with respect. So the window on the far side of the classroom beckoned, and each year for the next six years I got closer to that window.

Home life was busy; my mother had a child just about every two years or so. Dad built a tennis court and encouraged us to play: soon we were travelling on weekends to country tournaments. And as any country person knows, when you grow up on a farm, there's plenty of work to do. There was no mollycoddling or having things done for me. I just took it for granted that you helped — you did your chores, from making beds, washing up, and cleaning, to rounding up sheep, milking cows and fixing fences. There was no free Saturday afternoon to pass away the time: it was either organised sport or you helped. While I disliked milking, I became good with sheep and getting about on a horse. I sometimes rode to school, tethering Shanks, my pony, at the main gate outside the playground.

The farm was where I made my first business deal.

We had no pocket money — in fact there was little cash while my parents paid off a bank loan — and the only way I could make money was to pluck wool from dead sheep. It was smelly disgusting work, especially if the sheep had been dead more than a day. Longer than a few days and I couldn't face it. On went the gloves, handkerchief over the mouth and a deep breath. Sometimes the wool would come easily, and I'd stuff it into a cloth sack. Next time mum went to the nearest big town we'd drop by the wool broker, who'd purchase the contents of the sack.

By grade six I'd reached my goal at Wickliffe State School, number 948 and was sitting at the window — the view was the playground and I felt pretty special. I'd read all 1300 books in the school library, some a second time.

As often happens when life looks pretty good, my world fell apart. As an 11-year-old, I was top of the heap. Then came boarding school at a convent. I hated it. I was the youngest in a class of 39, almost twice the size of my old school. On my first weekend home,

I cried the whole time and begged my mother not to send me back. It did no good.

My salvation was sport — tennis in summer and netball in winter. At weekends I went home, also for holidays. My lasting memory of that school is the cooking — it was so bad I have never been able to buy a cabbage or cauliflower. For years I could not eat sausages.

After four years I again moved schools, this time to Kilbreda in the Melbourne suburb of Mentone, another Catholic school run by the same order of nuns.

We mixed only with other Catholic children, and at the twice-yearly school dances, our dresses were examined for modesty by the nuns. Padded bras were banned because they would excite boys beyond their level of control — and that would be disastrous. I wasn't quite sure what that meant. We were also checked for low necklines, or anything the least bit provocative. Patent shoes were considered bad because boys could look at the reflection and see up your skirt. There was a huge amount of strictness and tons of taboos.

The upside was that the head nun would talk about ex-students and their achievements. These were our role models: not housewives and husband-hunters, but women pursuing their own careers. It never occurred to me that my only option in life was to get married and have someone take care of me.

When I left school I had no clear picture of what I wanted to be. I had a vague idea I wanted to be a teacher — that's what my mother was, plus I'd seen a lot of teachers — and knew I wanted to go to university. At the age of six my mother told me I would be going to university. It was a powerful picture and, whenever anyone asked what I was going to do when I grew up, I said, 'Go to university.' As a six-year-old I had little idea what that meant, but I knew I would do it. But what would I study? Life at home on the farm gave me no role models. I couldn't be a farmer — women didn't become farmers in those days. I had no idea what it would look like to be a lawyer, a doctor, a businesswoman. So a teacher it was.

University was four years of finding out about the opposite sex, travel and growing up. At times, I was out of my depth, a naive country girl in the big city. It was a struggle to keep up. Some country people were completely swamped and left for home.

At boarding school my world had been mapped out from dawn till bedtime. Now, for the first time in my life, there was no one telling me what to do. And while some dived into drinking, smoking and sex, I eased into the social scene. I'd never had a boyfriend before university and I took to men like a duck to water. I dated seriously, sometimes three men a week. It was all pretty innocent, though — not even a hint of sex. And the Catholic university college had strict rules. We were allowed out only twice a week — once to 10pm and once to midnight. You had to fill in a form, naming your partner, what course he was doing, his address and where you were going.

Early in my second year I met Neil. He was tall and handsome, with a mischievous sense of humor. He'd gone off to study to become a priest, then thrown it in and enrolled for law at Melbourne University. I liked him immediately. Eight years later we were married.

Our first date was to Luna Park, which was a big surprise because I thought he was in love with another girl. I remember getting terribly nervous — I guess I was falling in love with him but didn't know it. We held hands on the roller coaster, a peck on the cheek at the end, nothing more. Sex outside marriage was a sin. It was high moral ground stuff.

A week after our first date Neil said he wanted to marry me. I was terrified by the idea. I was 18, in my second year of university, starting to get a taste of the world . . . I didn't want to get serious. I told him I wouldn't marry before I was 25. He said he'd wait.

Over the years, Neil was supportive and caring and became everything in my life — my father, my brother, my best friend. He was the rock of my life for many years to come, in work, travels, emotions and finances.

He never questioned my travels, which were all with girlfriends. In my uni days and early years of teaching I made half a dozen trips that took in New Zealand, Papua New Guinea, Fiji, Singapore, Malaysia, Thailand, Cambodia, Indonesia, and through some rugged parts of outback New South Wales and Queensland.

The reason behind the trips was just the adventure, doing something different. No one else was doing it. I didn't know anyone who'd hitch-hiked to Mt Isa or who'd been to Cambodia — I sometimes wanted to be the first to do interesting things, and that was the great stimulant for my travel.

At university I ignored my father's advice of 'do

your best'. I quickly learned what I needed to do to pass, and did just that. My social life was more important.

Of course you reap what you sow and, after three years, my marks were not good enough to keep me at Melbourne Uni with my friends. When it came time to do my year of teacher training, I qualified only for the suburban campus at Monash University, which in those days was a real comedown. Monash was brand new, with bare buildings and no trees; it was seen as inferior to Melbourne.

And there was no way out. For three years I'd been taking government money to be a student — my side of the deal was that I had to become a teacher for at least three years.

Once qualified, my first teaching job was even more isolated — the most remote high school in Victoria. Balmoral was a true one-pub town, with a general store, a garage and a smattering of people. The people were lovely, but for a 21-year-old girl sleeping in the lounge room of a two-room apartment, it was far from ideal. One morning I woke to find a cow's head poking through the loungeroom window, and got a hell of a fright.

The headmaster made it clear he didn't like me. Unfortunately, there had been a picture of me in the *Women's Weekly* social pages — a 21st of one of my university friends in Toorak — and this was published the day I arrived at the school. The first day of my first job, he walked into the staff room, flung the *Women's Weekly* across the table and made a derogatory comment about socialites and Toorak girls. Every weekend the staff fled town for Melbourne.

My next teaching post was in Benalla, in Victoria's north-east. One great highlight was learning to ski by following the local young farmers in their work coats down the slopes. No Austrian ski instructors here. This was learn to follow and collect the bruises!

All up I taught for three years then quit. I'd paid off my bond to the government and now wanted to get on with my life.

I left because I didn't see myself as a headmistress, and that's what I could expect if I got to the top. I also had little feedback, and the early feedback in Balmoral from the headmaster was negative and set the tone.

It wasn't until a couple of years after leaving that I got some great joy, when I ran into some of my ex-students from Benalla High School. 'Miss McIntyre,' said one boy, 'it's thanks to you we're at university.'

When I was a small child, the *National Geographic* arrived each month. I would always be the first to the magazine, to rip the wrapper off and find out where this month's journey took me. From a room in an isolated Australian farmhouse I'd find myself in Tibet, darkest Africa, the South American jungle, the Middle

HOME LIFE

East . . . I'd study the pictures and dream of visiting each place. At a tender age I caught the travel bug.

Travel gave me my first work experience; my first retail job, my first marketing job; it taught me about leadership, self-esteem, self-reliance; it taught me how to manage difficult situations, manage money, manage difficult people. Travel teaches you nothing's impossible — and that you must keep an open mind.

In fact, travelling is the best way to find out about both yourself and the world.

In 1971, after quitting teaching, I was ready for the epic journey, the long stay-away. And when you're young you know everything, but this one I got right. When my mother looked at my ticket at Melbourne Airport, she said: 'This ticket is from Melbourne to Calcutta. How are you going to get to London?'

'Mum, that's the purpose of the journey.' Business, like travel, is also an adventure.

I set off with my friends Pat and Eleanor on an adventure that took us through Hong Kong to India, Pakistan, Afghanistan, Iran, Turkey, Greece and eventually up to London.

Along the way we were almost attacked by a rampaging mob on an Indian train; we found the drug-addicted hippies in Kathmandu; had guns pointed at us by border guards; had our bus stoned by a mob in Iran after the driver accidentally killed a local; and we were ripped off by traders in a Turkish market. And we seemed to take it in turns to fall in love.

In Delhi I spent two weeks seeing an intelligent, wealthy Hindu man. He and his brothers had been educated in England and lived with their parents in a massive house with a dozen servants. He wined and dined me and finally, one Sunday, took me home to meet his family for lunch. And for his family, because I was white and not a Hindu, I was quite unacceptable. I was shunned and ignored — some looked through me, as if I wasn't there. I found it fascinating, my first experience of being discriminated against because of my skin color and race.

Each time one of us fell in love the others would chip away: 'Come on, we're going to London. If you think this is good, think how much better it's going to get.' And we kept going.

London circa 1971 was a mixture of pleasure and pain.

Much of the pleasure came from being the daughter of an Australian wool grower. Wool was still a big export to Britain and the wool brokers were generous with their hospitality. I had invitations to all sorts of parties and balls, to the races at Royal Ascot and the regatta at Henley-on-Thames.

This was my chance to meet England's famous upper class, the social elite. It was enormous fun and a wonderful time.

The pain was the money. Accommodation was expensive in London and we lived in a cheap, tatty place in — where else? — Earl's Court, a home-away-from-home for thousands of Australians and New Zealanders. We had a steady procession of Aussie visitors sleeping on couches and on our floor. I hated it.

But London gave me my first job outside teaching and a lesson on how to sell myself, plus the importance of persistence.

Australia House was a potential place for a job. I looked on noticeboards and found there was a job promoting Australian apples and pears. Ideal, I thought.

So I phoned the agriculture section and got a secretary. She told me not to bother applying. 'We've got 150 people on the waiting list for this. It's a very highly valued job. There are just so many Australian girls here and the waiting list is too long.'

It's always been a great challenge for me when everyone says something is too difficult. It is like an opportunity to prove to myself that I can do it.

So I kept calling back and finally, through sheer persistence, got put through to the man in charge of the department. I knew I had only a minute at best and had to sell myself well, so I had prepared my argument in a nutshell.

I said to him: 'My father is a wool grower and I've lived on a farm all my life and I understand Australian agriculture.' Although I knew about sheep and cattle, I knew nothing about Australian apples and pears. But I needed to get my foot through the door. 'Can I at least talk to you for five minutes and you can see if I'd be any good at doing this.'

I think due to sheer persistence he agreed. I went in and had an interview with him and persuaded him that I should be put at the top of the queue because of my vast experiences of Australian agriculture.

It worked. So I found myself with this job that paid £33 a week, where I got a car and accommodation when needed, and the chance to travel around England for several weeks promoting apples and pears. This compared with a job in Harrods at the time where friends were earning £13 a week.

After travelling through France and working as a nanny I returned to London. Among the dozens of letters that greeted me was a series of photographs of Neil in his academic gown. I showed them to my friends. They were astounded. 'Is this your boyfriend? Get back straight away! You're mad being here!'

I sensed they were right and booked a ticket to Australia. I phoned Neil and told him I was coming back. He was delighted. I knew at some point I had to come back, because I knew I had Neil waiting essentially for me — although he *did* say in the letter with the photograph that if I stayed away very much longer he would be seriously considering other 'options'. That was enough to make me pretty nervous because he'd been infinitely patient. Then I said I'd be a few weeks because I was going via Rome, Pakistan and the Philippines. He didn't mind. I was elated.

There was only one incident on the trip back that I'll record here. It was a scary incident and taught me to rely on one of the most important things each of us has — our instincts.

Even today I use my instincts in business. Not to make everyday decisions, but as an overall feeling, sometimes about people, sometimes situations.

Because instincts are sharpened experience, and instincts get better. In my travels I'd had a few close shaves. This was by far, in my mind, the closest.

HOME LIFE

It started innocently enough. I was travelling with Sue, who I'd met in London. We were hitch-hiking from London to Rome and coming into the city of Graz in Austria, when a man picked us up. His name was Karl, he seemed quite pleasant, and asked us where we were staying for the night. We said we didn't know, we hadn't decided — we hadn't booked anything, because it wasn't as though we were travelling from one five-star hotel to the next.

Sometimes we had lists of cheap hotels that other people had stayed at, sometimes it was sight unseen, then the bargaining would start about the price of rooms. But Karl had another idea: 'What I'll do is take you to dinner, and on to my parents. My family has a little cabin in the hills and you could stay there for the night.'

We declined but he insisted. It was their holiday house and they only went there on weekends. It was only 40 kilometres up in the hills. 'I'll drive you up after dinner,' he said.

What we decided — and we could speak very quickly in English to make plans — is we'd have dinner with Karl, check him out a bit more and, if we felt we could trust him, we'd do what he suggested. He was perfectly charming at dinner and afterwards drove us up to a little cabin, up a long winding road to a point where we could look down and in the distance see Graz. And the cabin itself was quaint: it had a huge open fireplace, big doonas on the beds. He lit the fire for us and said, 'I'll come and pick you up in the morning.' I had to be back in Graz to buy some shoes because my boots were completely worn through, so he was to pick us up at 9am.

We fell asleep innocently and comfortably, not imagining we were in any sort of danger whatsoever. The next morning we got up early, cleaned the place up, made the beds, swept the fireplace and waited. Quite soon after 9am, I said to Sue, 'I feel really nervous about this — something's happening here. I'm anxious.'

Sue was calm. 'It's only just after 9 o'clock. Of course he's coming. Don't worry.'

But for me, panic started to set in. There was no reason at all, it was purely intuitive. 9.15am. 9.20am. Sue was relaxed. I grew edgy.

'Sue, if he's not here by 9.30 we have to start walking.'

'No way. We can't.' We had suitcases and Sue had a lampshade she was taking to her sister in Italy. And there was no one on the road, a winding track up to weekend holiday cabins.

'We'll start walking and if he's coming towards us and there's no one in the car and it feels safe, we can come out of the bushes. Otherwise we're going to jump behind bushes when we hear a car so he won't be able to find us.'

'What do you think is happening?'

'I think this guy went around the pub last night. Right now, he's picking up all his mates and they're coming back here. We're totally vulnerable — there's no one else around, it's the middle of the week and they're going to rape us and possibly kill us and we'll never be heard of again because no one knows where

HOME LIFE

we are right now. The last time we contacted people was days ago by postcard.'

Sue kept saying this was ridiculous. But I had this terrible feeling that just got worse and worse.

We walked for more than an hour. Karl did not appear. And even Sue started thinking it was pretty strange: we had made a specific time.

Then we heard a car. I said, 'Sue, get behind the bushes.' We jumped behind bushes but it was a car going somewhere else — the only car we saw on the road to the cabin.

About three hours later — fortunately, it was a downhill walk — we finally got back to the turnoff from the main road. We were exhausted — this is the price paid for free travel — and crossed to the other side to wait for our next lift going our way.

A car pulled up straight away. We were getting in when a familiar car came towards us, slowed and took the cabin road turn. I happened to look up. 'Look, quickly.'

There, very close to us, facing us and about to turn — and they didn't see us — was Karl, and in his car were five other men. Sue and I quickly got in the car with our new driver and drove off speechless. I was as white as a ghost and just felt sick. There was no space for Sue and I in Karl's car.

I don't know what the intuition was. I don't know if it was a guardian angel. But to this day I really believe Karl meant us harm. We could have been raped, murdered and to this day been undiscovered.

Within six months of returning to Melbourne, in the following order, I began a new job, a new university course (commerce-law), got married and Neil and I bought our first house. It was settling down, big time!

My job was a stroke of luck, although it should be said that in 1972 there were jobs aplenty and it was a job-hunter's market.

I'd looked at school-teaching jobs and rejected the idea. Then someone suggested the Wool Corporation — being a country girl who grew up on a sheep farm, I'd be perfect.

So I walked into the foyer of the city building and told the receptionist I wanted a job. I had no idea what people did in city buildings. After some discussion she gave me the name of Lionel Ward, a man who was starting a new section, research economics.

I met Lionel two days later and we enjoyed an immediate rapport. Over the next seven years he gave me invaluable advice and was a sounding board for my ideas, questions and troubles. I learnt how to write reports, make presentations, run meetings, enter negotiations, analyse businesses and understand world economics. And I got to travel a great deal, meeting buyers in Europe who used Australian wool for clothing. It was a fantastic opportunity and one that gave me a great grounding in how a big business operates.

I ultimately left because I came across the limitations of being in big bureaucratic business — the reality was that you could only go so far. In your own business the sky was the limit. Being a woman in an organisation such as the Wool Corporation in the mid-1970s was no great advantage. The reality was it would take a long time to get to the top, if that was possible. And I became sick of the petty politics, laziness and bureaucracy that you can find in a big semi-government organisation.

I'd explain to my dad about wasted money, lazy people, misguided policies — and he'd be appalled, especially as he paid several cents in each dollar he made from his wool to keep the corporation going.

I jumped in a quite different direction by opening a shop. With my partner Liz Polk we imported top-quality fabrics, cushions, curtains, pottery and homewares. These goods were exclusive and expensive, but we felt there was a market and we were right. I was very green but learned quickly about retailing. We made money, albeit little, but moving into profit and staying there was no mean achievement. Shopkeeping is a tough way to make a living and I respect those who endure and prosper in retail a great deal.

But within two years I needed a change.

Within weeks of being married I began studying law and commerce at Melbourne University. It took six part-time years to finish the courses: I now had BA, B Com, Dip Ed — and then completed the preliminary year for a masters of business administration degree, which was in effect half an MBA.

At this time — and for a long time afterwards — I had the idea that the more you studied, the more successful you were, the more money you made.

And I liked money.

We bought an old house for $15,000 in the inner suburb of South Melbourne, an area that was becoming trendy. It smelt of stale urine and was revolting, but with big dreams and untold energy we took to the task of renovating the house.

For the first three months of our marriage — at the start of a Melbourne winter, mind you — we had no kitchen or bathroom, just a basin and toilet. If we wanted a shower we had to drive into the city to the building where Neil worked as a barrister.

We worked hard renovating the house — plaster, paint, wallpaper keeping us up till all hours. We both worked full-time, I studied at night and Neil did long hours as he began establishing his career. Our spare time was renovating or socialising. We were always on the go.

We sold the house two years later for $42,000. We were thrilled. Our next house was in Albert Park, again a big rambling property that needed a vast amount of work. We spent a year there, planning the renovations but never getting started. So we sold and made a 50 per cent profit. The property game looked great. We went to East Melbourne next, another big house.

Over this time we bought a farm. I still don't know why because we hardly went there. Then we bought a beach house at fashionable Portsea, spending most weekends there in a social whirl of parties, dinners and tennis.

We began going to charity balls, society cocktail parties, fashion parades, the races. Our pictures appeared in the social pages of newspapers. Life appeared glamorous, and to some extent it was. But underneath there were troubles.

Two years into our marriage I became pregnant. Then one night I had bad pains and began bleeding. I lost so much blood that by the time I got to hospital I needed several transfusions. I'd had a miscarriage. In a quite bizarre move I was put into a ward with women who'd just had their babies. My desolation and pain, amid all that joy and love, I'll never forget.

After the miscarriage it became difficult for me to conceive. I went on to fertility pills, but reacted so badly I had to give them away. We kept trying for children. For a few years I didn't buy new summer or winter clothes, thinking I might become pregnant. Each month, I thought I might be pregnant . . .

I never again became pregnant. I could not have children. This took some time to come to terms with and perhaps even today I am not over it. Every time I hear of cases of child abuse or parental neglect, I find it tough to deal with. I cannot believe people can produce children then neglect them, beat them, molest them, or allow near strangers into their home who abuse their children. It affects me greatly.

I was ill-prepared for marriage in many ways, not least of which that I couldn't cook or city shop. In the general store at Wickliffe shopping had been easy as there was only one brand of each product. I was not prepared for the choice in supermarkets.

Cooking I mastered. I had lessons and became competent in the fashionable foods of the early 1970s, a heavy French style. My speciality was beef wellington, a piece of fillet baked in pastry.

Cleaning didn't matter too much as our houses were always in the chaos of renovation.

Washing was OK, but ironing was a big problem. Neil was fastidious about his shirts. He showed me how to do them, cuff here, collar here. And even after half an hour on one shirt, I still couldn't get it right. He gave up and, thankfully, did his own ironing from then on.

Shopping. Well, my role model had been my mother who'd learned to feed a big family on very little money. Neil was an only child, used to the best. So the plain-brand tomato sauce was wrong (it was also, to be truthful, pretty disgusting). When I first cooked a chicken I came home with the biggest frozen chicken I could see — and it was half the price! Neil told me it was cheap because it was an old boiler — good only for making soup.

But I was ill-prepared in more serious ways and cracks began to show. It wasn't helped by the fact we worked so hard or the troubles we hit with money.

I realise now that planning, preparation and thought are essential for success. I'd done little thinking ahead of marriage. In fact I didn't really know what I was doing career-wise or life-wise. I had no goals. All I'd done is set 25 as an age before which I wanted to stay single. Now I'd passed 25, I could marry.

To an outsider our marriage may have looked great. And in many ways it was. But if you don't plan for something, anything can happen. We didn't plan.

I gave away too much responsibility. This was my fault, putting too much pressure and decision-making responsibility on Neil. Not only did he guide me on cooking, cleaning and ironing shirts, he would decide where I'd have my hair cut, what sort of image I'd have. He'd buy my clothes for me, my shoes, belts and bags. I had no confidence in my taste and tremendous confidence in his. The few times I actually bought clothes on my own, they always seemed a little wrong when I got home. So I gave up. It was easier to let my husband do all those things.

The worst aspect was money. We never seemed to have any. We were always looking at tax schemes. There was never any cash.

We had nice cars, a holiday home, big city house. But as I found out later, it was built on sand.

I found this hard to handle, but I'd left everything to Neil.

Growing up in the 1960s, women weren't encouraged to learn about shares or taxation. We weren't encouraged to be financially adept. At the time we bought our first house, single women weren't given mortgages by banks. Single men were.

Even though I knew I was good at handling money — I'd travelled overseas on my savings, and could make cash last — clearly Neil knew more than I did. He was from the city, so smarter. And he'd proved that when we bought and sold our first houses. I don't know if I even had a chequebook in the 1970s.

To all appearances we looked like a very together, confident couple, but actually I had very little confidence in myself and left every decision to my husband. That had really disastrous consequences when we finally split up after 11 years of marriage, because I was just totally lacking in the confidence — and moreover the skills — about all sorts of basic things in my life. Even to this day I'm still doing some things for the first time, like some things around my house that I'd never had to do.

I let Neil do everything with money and I abrogated my responsibility totally. That's the best way I can put it. I didn't contribute. And so I was equally as responsible for our marriage failure and the lack of money. I learned the hard way.

6
TICKET TO RIDE

The number of times we succeed is based on the number of times we try

written in my diary

Direct selling is a bit like a train journey. When people join Pola or any other direct-selling company they buy their 'ticket', a starting kit that costs a few hundred dollars — the price of a new pair of quality shoes. Everyone gets the same 'ticket'; it provides the same samples, manual, videos, seminars and audio tapes, even the same travel opportunities.

And when people get on that train, they can stay aboard as long as they like. Some leave early, others stay for a while, some keep going all the way along the line. And some buy their ticket and never get on!

After four days of euphoria in Japan, I flew back to my reality. I was standing alone on the platform, my ticket in hand. In front of me was the Pola train. It was full of empty seats.

Those first weeks and months were tough. There was little financial reward. I was paid a $300 weekly retainer, plus a percentage of the turnover of the business. If I recruited anyone, the turnover would go up, and so would my income. Yet it was very little of very little. I was earning a fraction of what I could make in a corporate job. And there were plenty of disappointments.

At home our financial crisis reached its peak. In my diary I started keeping notes of how much we spent because money had become so tight. One morning I opened a letter that showed the size of our mortgage. It was huge. I had no idea we owed so much and was stunned.

For some time the money coming in was not enough to meet what we owed. Neil had entered several tax-minimising schemes, but these had gone badly wrong and cost much more than they saved. We were forced to sell our home and the marriage came to an end. I was distinctly angry, first with my husband, then later with myself. (It took time for me to realise I was equally to blame because I let Neil do all the finances.) With only a few pieces of furniture and two weeks' rent paid in advance, I moved into a small flat. Apart from my car I had no other assets.

It was damaging, sad, like my life was splitting in two. We'd known each other for 18 years. There was no screaming or yelling, just the sad acknowledgment of the end of our marriage. The main relationship for my whole adult life was with Neil, so a huge part of my existence was really dying. It was disturbing and very hard to handle, but the relationship just had nowhere to go. I had shed a skin. I had to start again.

The break-up of an emotional relationship is very difficult. Even if people leave willingly it's a very traumatic experience. It's like a death really because a person you've relied on, depended on and been with for so long is just simply not there. And so all those things you get used to, the small things you get used to doing together, are just not available any longer and all of a sudden you're on your own.

And it left me lonely and frightened because I was used to having the security of Neil's opinions, particularly as he made so many decisions about my life. He had so dominated my decision-making that when we split — ridiculous as it seems today — my biggest immediate worry was what was I going to wear for summer. I couldn't do it. I rang Neil and said, 'Come and help me'. I couldn't even choose my lipstick color — and I was building a cosmetics company.

My confidence and self-esteem were at rock bottom.

Work was proving tough, and many times I just wanted to throw it all in. After all, I hadn't committed much money to the project, so financially there was little to lose. And it wasn't long before I discovered that I was following in the footsteps of two other women. Both had been recruited by John Taylor to run Pola, both had been to Japan — and after a few weeks more, both had quit because the job was just too hard. Today, I thank Taylor for not telling me about these women during his pitch for me to set up Pola; it was a negative that had no place in the negotiations. But of course, I did find out. And I faced the same hurdles: the product was expensive, people didn't understand direct selling and there were long, long hours to be put in with little to show at the end of the day.

But I knew there was a possible future with Pola. I had seen the size and scope of the business in Japan, I knew there were huge possibilities. And I grabbed the chance and held on. It was my rock in a storm and I wasn't going to let go.

My vision was vague, but I could see and touch the network of salespeople John Taylor had built in his pottery and textile businesses. The Japan visit had given me huge confidence in Pola Inc. And I was using the products and knew they were first class. This was an opportunity to build something from nothing — and in my perilous financial state it was one of the few businesses I could be involved in. I had no assets so I couldn't get a bank loan. So, tied into my long-term vision, becoming financially independent became a specific goal.

I took small steps at first: learning to sell, learning to recruit people, learning to make business appointments, learning to supply stock. I was learning, listening, taking notes. Repeating them back. Practise, practise, practise. Once you know it so well you don't have to think about it, you can move to other things.

John Taylor provided fantastic support. As a mentor and guide he was invaluable, although it was like starting all over again. All my study and qualifications meant nothing — my teacher was someone who'd left school at 15. But I needed his skills.

He insisted the Pola division remain separate from

the pottery and textile divisions, so none of the saleswomen in those areas were given cosmetics to sell. I had to recruit my own people. His advice was always helpful. I got into the habit of writing sayings in the front of my work diary, a habit I still have today.

In the early years I used to regularly look at the following:

- Winning isn't everything, it's the only thing
- You can rise to the height of your dreams
- You never fail until you stop trying
- Setbacks are an integral part of success
- You are allowed to look back at the past but you are not allowed to stare
- Let your dreams take command, not your regrets

For the first time I heard motivational speakers. The first seminar I went to had an American speaker and even though it was a little bit hypey and wide-eyed, it amazed me. I had never heard anyone delve into the question of attitude, of being optimistic about life. I'd just never read anything about this or studied it or even heard anything about it; it certainly wasn't part of my tertiary education.

Some speakers, such as American Tom Hopkins, were sales trainers: he raised qestions on how to deal with rejection, how to close a sale, how to treat objections, the importance of language. He explained you should never ask anyone to 'sign a contract', but use phrases such as 'let's fill this in now'.

I started reading motivational books, going from book to book. There was always something fascinating to read and it was extremely helpful because I had so many doubts about what I was doing. Plus I had to inspire recruits to counter the same objections and challenges I faced. They needed motivating too. There were books on attitude, spirit, motivation, goal-setting, people overcoming the odds. I knew nothing of these things. A lover of fiction, my reading habits changed forever as I locked into this source of outside strength.

A few weeks after returning from Japan I hired my first recruit, Maggie, a schoolteacher who a friend said might be interested in making some extra money. She proved a great success, averaging twice the sales I made. And for me, a picture was forming — if I could recruit a large number of people who were better than I was, Pola would bloom. Maggie lasted only a year before marrying and leaving Melbourne. Another to get off the train.

Almost every day I was travelling out to Mulgrave from South Yarra — 40 minutes in the car each way, more in heavy traffic — picking up my products and visiting houses all around Melbourne — Melton in the west, Frankston in the south and the Dandenongs in the east. I kept making links, and kept networking and it all started to grow.

Even though I'd travelled a lot, mostly overseas, I soon realised my social networks and life had been quite sheltered; I was going to suburbs I'd never visited, meeting completely different people and seeing another side of life.

In my first six months I recruited 30 people, still working my way down the list of potential customers and recruits that I'd started on day one. A recruit's income was 30 per cent of anything they sold. If they (person A), in turn, recruited someone else (person B), person A would earn 35 per cent of what they sold. If person A recruited two people or more, they earned 35 per cent of their own sales plus 2 per cent of person B and person C's sales. At Pola, while person A could make money from other people's sales, 2 per cent was not very much. The financial incentive was to *make sales yourself*, a system I designed for that reason, to give more to the saleswoman who was selling the most.

For me, however, it was the more recruits the better. In the front of my diary, in big letters, I wrote: 'Do something about recruiting every day.' And I did. For the next 15 years.

Each day I had a list of presentations my team was doing, and each day I'd go to one of their presentations. I would help out then recruit from those presentations — and this went on day in, day out.

In addition to these and my own presentations I would train people — I had notes that Pola gave me, translated from Japanese, which I put into a training manual. My teaching skills proved handy. In fact, no skills I'd picked up went unused: some time, somewhere, every one was applied at Pola. I found I knew more than I knew I knew.

There were regular meetings of my team, generally in my apartment, mostly on selling, recruiting and presentations.

It is said you end up teaching what you have to learn most and I was in the middle of what I had to learn most. And I felt like I was doing a degree in sales, recruiting and motivation. And putting it into practice every day.

It was effort and energy, getting out and doing it, doing it, and doing it again until I was so good I didn't have to think about it.

Business got better and I started travelling interstate, running training meetings, motivational meetings. It was exciting.

I began building teams in other states. And I was buoyed along by people I'd introduced to the business. I focused on the figures. In my first year I worked 70-hour weeks and took only a week off work. I earned a modest $27,000.

Back in my apartment, in my personal life, I still felt lost and lonely. But I think I began to find myself, who I was, what I wanted to do. No more facades, straight to the nitty gritty.

And that meant hard work, four and five sales presentations a week at whatever time I had to do them, according to other people's schedules, plus training, recruiting and building the central core of a business. The picture, the vision of what I was building became clearer, yet at times I had enormous doubts and wanted to stop. In those times John Taylor's success story was an inspiration to me in itself.

And I knew it was really up to me if I wanted to achieve anything in my life. I had to take responsibility. It was a hard, long lesson before I learned that.

From the second year I started travelling interstate a lot, about 30 times a year. Some trips were unbelievably frustrating. I would pre-arrange to meet someone who sounded really good on the phone. I'd have a long talk to them, send information, they'd make commitments about starting the business, then I'd fly there and sometimes there'd be the message waiting at the hotel, sorry, couldn't make the meeting, decided to do something else. Those were awful visits. I have never forgotten a Saturday night alone in a motel in the New South Wales country town of Wagga Wagga, where the person I'd flown up to visit left such a message.

But I was so determined to succeed I saw such setbacks as part of the process. Like building any business, you are going to be let down by people, let down by events, let down by the economy and all these things, but unless you just keep working at it you simply won't make it

There were enormous frustrations — postponed sales meetings, abandoned interviews with potential recruits — but I just kept working though it because, having made this commitment, there was no way I was going to let it fail.

And the numbers began to fall into place. In 1984 Pola recruited 97 people, the next year it jumped to 173, in 1986 it slipped slightly to 160 but that was still three new sales people a week. And as 1987 rolled around, my vision was slowly coming together. I wanted to recruit a record number of people for the year, plus hold as many of the existing team as possible.

After five years of struggle, everything seemed to be going so well.

7
A TOUGH CALL

The greatest risk of all is to take no risk at all
written in my diary

I've always enjoyed dinner parties. Over good food and wine, they are a chance to catch up with friends, meet new people and exchange ideas.

Sometimes there's the odd bombshell, too. In midwinter 1987 I got the first scent of trouble.

I was in Brighton: the veal was beautiful, the chardonnay cold and I was tucking into my food when one of four men at the table mentioned that his neighbor was going into business with John Taylor.

The alarm bells started ringing. Loudly.

'Yes, he's got into some new cosmetics deal,' the dinner party guest said across the table. 'You probably know about it.'

'Well, things are pretty busy,' I said, smiling. But

inside, I was in turmoil. My heart was racing. I had no idea what he was talking about.

What was going on?

The next day I confronted John Taylor.

'I hear you're involved in a new cosmetics business. Can you tell me what's going on?'

'I can't talk about it right now, I'm afraid, Marcia.'

And he wouldn't say any more. In fact he was downright secretive.

So I went sleuthing.

I'm not especially proud of what I did next, but I had little choice. And I'm certainly not ashamed. Besides, hadn't the man himself said, 'Whatever it takes'?

One night after Taylor had gone home, I went into his office to see if I could find any clues about what was going on. There was nothing on the desk, but in the rubbish bin I found some shorthand notes written by his personal assistant. I pocketed them.

But on my knees looking through the bin I mistakenly unplugged a power point. I'm sure Taylor found it because, from then on, despite a few more midnight searches, I found only innocent information in the bin.

I took the notes to a friend who read shorthand and she 'translated' them. And the truth emerged.

Taylor's plan was to have a tie-in deal with the Jenny Craig weight-loss business. He would provide them with skin-care products and cosmetics. The weight-loss company would put its name on the labels and when women went to lose weight, they would be offered products. Some would even be given away in promotions and as rewards for losing weight.

Meanwhile, according to the shorthand notes, I would continue to lead the direct-selling of Pola.

I was aghast.

The plan just didn't make sense. First, I wondered whether women would actually buy any cosmetics with 'Jenny Craig' emblazoned on them. Cosmetics companies spend millions each year on advertising to give their products a glamorous, luxurious and sexy image. Why would someone use a product that said: 'I am trying to lose weight'?

But, more importantly, putting Pola products into Jenny Craig would kill the direct sales business. There was only a small market for the expensive Pola products and only one way to sell them. You couldn't expect the direct sales business to survive if a mass-market sales plan went ahead.

As I thought about the plan, pieces of the jigsaw began to fit into place. All the meetings I had not attended — including a visit by the Japanese: I now knew their purpose.

The shorthand notes revealed that the consortium planning the Jenny Craig tie-in had extensive contact with Japan and contracts for the deal had been prepared.

I asked friends with marketing experience if they thought I was being paranoid. Could you have two Pola businesses in the same market? Would the image change with a Jenny Craig tie-in? All agreed there were significant problems.

The question was: were the Japanese aware I didn't know? Because if that was the case and they'd agreed with Taylor that I needn't be informed, then I didn't

A TOUGH CALL

have a future with Pola. I might as well have packed up and left.

So should I telephone them? Fly to Japan? What should I do?

I thought about my passion for Pola, what I'd created, and I wanted to protect it. Had I not been enthusiastic I would have bowed out at that stage. I could have readily got a job in the corporate area, especially in the cosmetics industry. But there was no way I was going to walk away from Pola without a fight. Yet at the same time I felt distinctly uncomfortable.

I was in direct conflict with my boss, mentor, teacher, a man who had given me a great opportunity. Our visions for Pola were obviously different. It wasn't as if I had a blind ambition to run the company. I found myself in the situation because of a lack of communication.

I decided to fax the Japanese, tell them I'd just found out about this deal, had no knowledge of it and from a marketing standpoint it was a bad idea. I listed the reasons, told them if they did this they would kill the direct-selling business and I would leave. It was a tough do-or-die fax and I didn't know which way it would go.

The minute Pola Japan got the fax someone was on the phone deeply concerned. They had no idea I was unaware. The contract they had was based on my being fully aware. They were deeply upset.

Pola tore up the contract and said it would not produce goods for the consortium, which in effect ended the business relationship between Pola and John

Taylor. Then Pola contacted me again. Would I run the business?
    OK.

8
THE BUCK STOPS HERE

> *A diamond is a chunk of coal
> that has made good under pressure*
>
> written in my diary

A few days later I phoned John Taylor — the conversation was far from pleasant. Suffice to say that what followed was not a friendly changeover and my first experience of real business conflict.

And it wasn't the only unpleasant thing.

His personal assistant promptly left the company, taking her valuable experience and knowledge. This was a nightmare. I still had to travel and train people and there was a huge vacuum in administration.

The consortium decided to go ahead with its Jenny Craig tie-in using another company's cosmetics products. Within days John began trying to recruit my best saleswomen.

Worse, I discovered the Pola business was running at a loss. It had been in the red for *every* month of its operation. It was a big lesson, one I should have learned from my marriage — watch the money. Yet for five years I'd been promoting a great product but had no idea about its business viability. I had entrusted that to someone else.

It was a case of not only keep your eye on the money, but keep your eye on the big picture.

It was normal practice for a foreigner running a Japanese company to have either a Japanese person in the firm looking after the accounting or a trusted international accountancy firm supervising the books.

John Taylor had used an accountancy firm and I inherited the system.

The accountants were no doubt spooked by the company losses and immediately stepped up their diligence. The man in charge was almost obstructive — he had to countersign every cheque and began to query basic business decisions I made, such as using couriers. Couriers were fundamental to the distribution of Pola goods.

I simply didn't have time for endless meetings with the accountant to justify day-to-day expenses.

I was spending a lot of time calming my team, some of whom were nervous about The Man's sudden departure. I told them everything would be fine, but in my heart I didn't know. My old boss was in direct competition, trying to recruit my sales team, the business was running at a loss, I had a hostile accountant and a head office that didn't know what was going on. They had no experience of a Caucasian female — and many Japanese men frowned on women being involved in senior levels of business. Pola, despite being the third

THE BUCK STOPS HERE

biggest cosmetics company in Japan, had no women at executive level. Why should they trust me? Especially as I'd worked with John, who'd misled them.

I felt vulnerable, and had a sales team that relied on me to give them confidence.

When I looked into the accounts I could see expenses were the big problem. The equation was simple: they were bigger than the company's income, so Pola was running at a loss. With sound financial management — and keeping my eye on expenses — the company had the potential to run at a profit. But it was tight.

After three months the company turned the corner and made a small profit. Only one person out of 1000 on my books left Pola to join John Taylor's consortium. She invested a few thousand dollars in a kit and left not long after. The project died within three months.

I told the Japanese I was not prepared to continue if I wasn't given sole cheque-signing rights. There was no way I could build the business with a petty bureaucrat overseeing my every decision and needing endless meetings for me to explain every dollar. They agreed.

It was a big vote of confidence and allowed me to get on with business. Over the next few months we slipped back into loss, but it was much smaller than before. And as I began to take control of the office systems, small profits began to appear.

In 1987, Pola lost $130,000. Within six months I'd turned that around into a monthly profit. By 1989, we made a profit of $130,000.

I flew to Japan for the annual convention feeling pretty pleased with myself. I'd set a budget of sales growth of 35 per cent, which had been just far too high. It had been a goal, a target, and in achieving 20 per cent growth I thought we'd done pretty well. We were in profit and growing.

But when I reached Japan I was completely ignored for the first three days — there were no one-on-one meetings — and people looked through me as if I was glass.

I couldn't work it out and after three days my sense of humour was wearing thin. And when I finally met members of the international department they expressed horror that I hadn't achieved my 35 per cent business-growth target for my first year.

It was a clear lesson. When dealing with Japanese, be conservative. Don't promise more than you can do. What they call a 'goal' or a 'budget' or a 'target' is what needs to be achieved.

In future years, as Pola grew, even through the recession of the early 1990s, I was far better off when targets were exceeded. Then it showed what a good year we'd had — and I would collect a bonus.

With the departure of John Taylor my role changed. I went to fewer presentations and most recruits who joined the company were brought in by existing team members. In turn they built their networks, a system where they earned a small percentage of anything their recruits sold.

Some women built phenomenal teams which effectively became divisions of the company, the women divisional managers. My role was to supply products, training, support and encouragement — and endless energy.

And even though the product was expensive it wasn't socio-economic demographics that decided sales, it was the quality of the sales teams. At various times we had extremely strong sales in the small Queensland town of Emerald and in New Plymouth, a small city in New Zealand.

Each year the number of consultants increased, each year the profit went up. Annual sales growth while I was at Pola averaged 30 per cent. In 1995 the company moved into an office-warehouse in Prahran, opened by Premier Jeff Kennett and the Australasian division was Pola's fastest-growing overseas business for several financial years. By 1997 there were more than 4700 consultants on our books in Australia and New Zealand run from Melbourne by a staff of seven, including myself.

And fifteen years after knocking on Mary-Ellen's door nervously clutching a cardboard box and a briefcase, it was time to quit.

Book Three

Would You Rather
Buy a New Pair of
Shoes
or
a Business?

If you think education is costly, try ignorance

If you have to be anything, be fabulous

Never lose sight of the big picture

9
THE SECRETS OF HIGH-HEELED SUCCESS

Success depends not on what you are able to do but what you are willing to do

written in my diary

The secrets of success are not really so secret. In fact, aspects of successful planning and achievement are centuries old and have been well publicised. No amount of technological change will *ever* alter these basic human realities, however much technology changes the structure and style of our lives and careers.

But for women there's something more: there's a need to bring on success, to make a conscious decision about the way we think, something that many men don't need. Men's desire for success is in-built, something they must get through their mother's milk or through locker-room osmosis. The effects of this we'll discuss in chapter 12. Many women get 'stuck' in helpmate jobs; they are the personal assistants to the managing directors, which in some cases is just the wrong way round. It's a crucial question: how many women of merit and mettle do you know who could handle bigger, tougher, more satisfying roles *but don't do it?*

I am one of a small group of Australian women who can honestly say that I'm financially independent, that I've built a multi-million dollar business and created work opportunities for thousands of people, and that I'm regarded by many businessmen as an equal. Unfortunately, there are far too few of us. I earnestly hope that over time this will change dramatically.

Success, by definition, is achieving what you set out to do, whether it be in your business life or personal life. This could mean competing in the Olympics, saving money for a holiday or shedding five kilograms in weight. When you achieve your goal you feel an inner reward.

And it's a very personal thing. What one person sees as a success in life someone else may not see that way at all. All each of us can do is work out what we want and strive for it.

Some people think success is easy, perhaps because it's flashed in front of us every day. There are musicians, sportsmen and actors making extraordinary money in a short time; young business people with inventions, especially in the computer age, quickly building companies and gaining huge power. But they are rare among the total talent-bank of musicians, sportsmen, actors and business people. Only a small percentage of these people really make it.

Yet sometimes it appears to us that success is

something you can get very easily — just get a good idea and make it happen.

This just isn't true. Success is really difficult. Very few people find it easy to be successful.

There is, however, a five-step formula for success, which I will develop in the next five chapters:

- Step one is having some idea of what you want to be, want to do, and what makes you happy
- Step two is to set goals to achieve those aims
- Step three is working smart to achieve those goals
- Step four is persistent, consistent effort
- Step five is a combination of factors that add up to attitude

Over the years I've given a great deal of thought to why some people succeed and some fail. I've looked for a pattern in successful people's upbringings, but there isn't one. There are great success stories of people from really sad and impoverished backgrounds; and often in middle or upper-middle class families people go on to drugs and dream away their lives.

Likewise, money is something people often strive for. Many people measure success in money — from a bank balance to the sort of car you own. But money doesn't buy you the most important thing in life. Stories of misery with money are well documented. Happiness is the key — whether you are poor in financial terms or rich in financial terms, it is much more important that you wake up each day to a happy life.

And common to all successful people is a great sense of self-reliance. When it comes to the crunch they are not dependent on the opinions of other people but prepared to be individuals, to tough it out, see it through. They are prepared to go for their goals and dreams.

10
SECRET # 1
DREAMS AND PASSION

Where do you want to go today?

Microsoft screen saver

In June 1982 I had a vague dream about Pola — a lot of people working with me, a growing business around the country, a financial success. Yet the vision was clouded by friends who sowed seeds of doubt — and much of what they said made sense.

The product was unknown. There was no advertising budget. It was expensive, putting it in competition with the world's most exclusive cosmetics. It was Japanese and 'not suitable' for Caucasian skin. I knew nothing about selling, let alone direct selling. I knew nothing about cosmetics, except as a consumer. My friends thought of me as an economist, not an expert in skin care. All true, relevant, telling points. And unhelpful.

Dreams are not meant to be rational, logical and

safe. A vision of life, be it personal or business, is for the brave and the daring.

And in 1982 I needed a vision. Until then I'd had only fuzzy pictures about life — mostly about a happy, contented marriage — but when life with my husband began to fall apart there was no real dream to keep us together.

I now realise that the only way you can succeed in life is to have a goal, a vision of how you would like to be at various stages of your life; like halfway through your life, towards the end, etc.

This isn't taught in school or university. People gain lots of skills, but they don't learn about how they want their life to be. And this is the key issue that needs to be addressed with young people.

As a teacher, I loved French, English and history. But if I was a teacher again, I would rather be teaching a course called 'How to make the most of your life'. It wouldn't mean everyone would learn the same set of values, but they would be taught the key skills required to design a successful life.

I once did a three-day course that began with the question: 'What does it mean to be a human being?' As the coach of this group went around the room of 150 people, no one was really able to stand up and define what it meant to be a human being. That was fascinating. Here we were, all of us at various ages and stages of our lives, yet no one knew. I suppose that is some sort of indication that most of us meander through life without questioning what it means to be a human being, and what it means to be a successful human being.

DREAMS AND PASSION

A successful human being is one who achieves what he or she sets out to do, so if you don't have a goal or have no idea of what you want to do, then you've got little chance of being successful.

Lewis Carroll's *Alice In Wonderland* sums it up nicely:

'Would you tell me, please, which way I ought to go from here?' said Alice.

'That depends a good deal on where you want to get to,' replied the Cat.

And as the Chinese saying goes: 'Every journey begins with a single step.' But if you are wanting to go south, a step north is counter-productive.

As strange as it seems, it appears to me that most people go through life without ever having a picture of a possible journey, no concept of what really makes them happy. And without vision there can be no goals — and without goals there can be no measure of personal success or fulfilment or progress.

Simply summed up, clarity is power.

Passion is one of the world's most powerful forces. It can be kindled at any time, at any age. It puts us above the ordinary and is essentially the thing that keeps us truly alive. Passion is about the athlete who gets up at five every morning for years hoping for Olympic selection. It is about hard work, clarity, commitment and faith. It lets you absorb loneliness, exhaustion and a lack of gratitude.

Passion was the engine that let me build Pola, driven by my belief in the product and the vision I had for the company. It let me work 70-hour weeks, week after week, travelling across Melbourne at all hours, making 30 trips a year across Australia and New Zealand, for at first little financial reward. I had no advertising budget but competed with the world's leading cosmetics companies. I travelled thousands of kilometres to meet would-be consultants, some of whom failed to show — but despite the disappointments my passion instilled a commitment to making Pola work. People kept rejecting my offers to show them the product — but I had faith that it would make it in the marketplace. Tired and alone in my apartment at the end of the day I could look to my vision, what I was trying to achieve, and rekindle my passion for the next day. Passion proved so energising that it helped me overcome all obstacles.

More than a few times my friends thought I was crazy, but it was my very passion that helped me ignore this.

Author and friend Charles Kovess defines passion thus: A source of unlimited energy which enables one to achieve extraordinary results.

And he's spot on. Passion may last a short time or it may last a lifetime. And with passion and a dream, you can begin to plan your success.

11

SECRET # 2
THE BEST
LAID PLANS

Setbacks are an integral part of success

written in my diary

In April 1995 I decided to run the Melbourne marathon. I had six months to prepare for the 42-kilometre race and, because I ran five kilometres each morning, I was confident that my basic fitness was good.

Within days, the first part of my plan began to unravel.

I was told that the date of the marathon had been changed and was not October but June. Instead of six months to prepare I had just over six weeks. I was keen to press ahead and phoned a friend who had run several marathons and we discussed a training schedule of running each day, building up the distance each week. It was a tight schedule that looked like this:

	Mon	Tue	Wed	Th	Fri	Sat	Sun	Week's total Km
Week One	11	5	5	10	5	10	5	51
Week Two	15	5	5	10	5	10	5	55
Week Three	20	5	8	10	5	12	5	65
Week Four	20	5	8	10	5	12	5	70
Week Five	25	8	8	10	8	12	9	80
Week Six	25	8	8	10	8	12	9	80

At the end of week five all was going well; I'd run each day and ticked off the target every morning.

On Monday, six days before the race, I went to lunch at Melbourne's Sofitel Hotel for the inaugural Telstra Victorian Businesswoman of the Year Award. Like hundreds of other women I'd been nominated, had sent in details of the company and its corporate structure, and had been interviewed by a panel of judges. After that I'd thought little about the award — I was very busy as it was close to the end of the financial year. My expectations of winning anything were very low — in fact, I was so busy I hadn't done my hair before rushing to the lunch.

When the awards in the four categories were announced I was staggered to be named the winner of the best company employing less than 100 people — Pola's 4700 consultants were served by a team of only seven people at head office. When I was named as the overall winner to go to the national finals, I was almost speechless.

The award was stunning for me and for Pola. I was interviewed on radio and television, and articles appeared in newspapers and magazines. People I hadn't seen for years rang or sent congratulatory faxes. Friends

THE BEST LAID PLANS

sent flowers. I received dozens of invitations to lunch and dinner. Pola consultants found renewed interest among their customers and sales went up. I felt I could celebrate. All the years of hard work were finally being recognised and each evening I went to dinner, had a few drinks and enjoyed myself. I ran most mornings — but not enough.

The day before the marathon, as I was set to go to another party, the realisation hit me. The marathon was tomorrow. I'd planned to run 80 kilometres for the week but had managed just 30. Common sense told me to cancel, but I couldn't resist. I had to run.

The following day we started in St Kilda Road at the edge of the city. There were thousands of people and the buzz was exhilarating, enough to carry me for the first 10 kilometres. At 15 kilometres I was going OK. Then things began to get a bit tough. At 21 kilometres, as those running the half-marathon stopped, having reached their goal, I ploughed on. At the 30-kilometre mark I felt I would die and friends who saw me there said later I looked half-dead. But once past 30 kilometres I found new energy and my emotions carried me on. But not far.

At 34 kilometres I simply fell on to a police car, unable to go on. A bus picked me up and with other non-finishers drove us to the finish line. I took a taxi home without a medal. My dented pride was further bruised as the people I'd trained with in those early weeks all finished the race.

When I got home I lay in a hot bath and was surprised that I seemed to be OK. The next day I went into the office and, while a little stiff, felt fine, certainly well enough to resume the celebratory round.

Two days later it hit me. After lunch I began to feel strange, the start of three weeks of nausea and headaches. I saw several doctors and still felt no better. When I went to the national Businesswoman of the Year finals in Sydney two weeks later I was still ill and spent most of the time in bed in my hotel room. Eventually I saw a chiropractor who told me my body was dangerously dehydrated and everything I'd been taking had just made it worse. After a few days on a new diet I was back to normal.

The whole exercise was a big lesson in planning. If you break down a goal into steps, be sure you finish every step, because if you don't, things go wrong. In my case I should have shelved the aim of running the whole marathon when I failed to stick to the plan in the last week. I would have saved myself weeks of ill health.

Achieving my goals step by step gives me enormous happiness and encouragement. This applies equally in my business and personal lives. Even sometimes the frustration put in the way of achieving those goals can become points of accomplishment when you turn them around.

The most important thing about a successful plan is to have the end in mind. If I can envisage what I am trying to achieve, what it will look like, feel like, then I am part-way there.

Other factors that are essential are:

- The goal should be clear
- The goal should then be worked backwards into achievable chunks, year by year, month by month, day by day
- The goal should be in writing
- The goal must be realistic

And like my marathon experience, if circumstances change, goals should change. Goals should be both focused and flexible.

I've certainly had a greater commitment to my goals by being able to believe them, feel them, see them, touch them because if they get too far out of reach or they are not attractive, it becomes very hard to maintain a commitment.

In dealing with head office in Tokyo, I continually hit cultural hurdles and, in my 27 trips to Japan, failed to come close to understanding my colleagues as individuals. There was a huge cultural gap that was extraordinarily difficult to bridge. Yet we had the same goals for Pola Australia — to expand the business — and that was enough to keep the company on track. And while I was working with people on a very impersonal level, which is typical of Japanese companies and something I found difficult at first, it ultimately *didn't matter* because the goal was the same.

I think most of us would like the same sort of things: the perfect relationship, a large amount of money, or financial freedom of choice at least. But the reality is: What is possible given the circumstances? What can I really achieve?

If I set realistic objectives and targets, I have more happiness and fewer frustrations than if my goals are just unattainable. Of course, some people achieve goals that appear unattainable — but in their mind they've worked out a strategy or plan to achieve those goals.

And successful people not only run their life with a purpose, they have systems to help them reach their goals. Equally a business must have good systems. A great example is McDonald's, where structures and systems are the hamburger chain's great strength. And systems must be in writing — and be changed if required. If you have systems in your business then you can work on your business.

When I began at Pola there were no systems. I had to start from scratch, aided only by a few notes from Pola Japan which had been translated from Japanese and their relevance to Australia was limited.

The first system needed was how to do presentations. This was based partly on trial and error and partly on watching John Taylor and some of his other employees in action.

Over some months it became clear which plans worked best and it became easier to give each person who joined the company a plan that worked. The hard part was getting people to follow the plan. I was always fascinated by people who joined the company, followed the plan, became successful, then decided they wanted to do it their own way and they failed. And despite their system not working as well, they preferred to do it their way and fail.

A second key system was the ordering and delivery of products. This was an essential cog in the wheel of

THE BEST LAID PLANS

Pola. Customers would be lost — and disillusioned consultants leave — if goods were either not in the warehouse or not dispatched promptly. This was a matter of good management and, with computerisation, for the most part became sweetly efficient.

The equation was simple: when we discovered a good system we kept repeating it, and when we found a bad system we avoided it. This made business, and life, much easier.

The third key plan for the company's development was recruiting, and this had eight main aspects to it:

- Sales presentations were the main source of new recruits and we kept managers (those with four or more recruits in their team) informed of the number of presentations held and the number that were coming up, and of the names of possible recruits who attended the presentations
- Meetings were held around Australia and New Zealand that drew new people, often resulting in multiple recruits
- A magazine was published each month, not only to keep consultants informed about the company, but to attract potential consultants
- Incentives were organised, especially overseas travel, that were often based on the number of people recruited over a period of time
- Training seminars were developed to encourage consultants to recruit more people
- Publicity raised the profile of Pola and drew more people to the company, either to use the product

or to join; the publicity that went with the Businesswoman of the Year Award was very beneficial
- My public speaking proved an effective way of raising Pola's profile and I made time for engagements across Australia and overseas

The mix of the above often changed and many experiments were made. I was always prepared to rewrite the plan if I thought it would improve.

In some companies there is a reluctance to try something new. At the Wool Corporation I found some aspects of the business had descended into such a bureaucratic routine that people were unsure what the goal actually was or what was the best way to achieve it. They'd forgotten what they did things for.

So when someone says, 'We've always done it like this' I am horrified. It was not an acceptable phrase at Pola. New systems that work better should always be considered and developed. The rules must be firmly set, but flexible enough for change. And often that requires great strength of character because it's often easier for things to stay as they are.

One of the key aspects of my planning is to pick the eyes out of all the good ideas around me. If I want to decorate a house, I get ideas from the best decorators; if I want to learn about money, I go to the best financial planners; if I want to learn about selling, I go to the best salespeople and learn those skills.

If we could get skills in all parts of our lives from the experts, we'd be in pretty good shape because we'd be able to be the best at many things.

It sounds obvious and simple, but so often people

depend on the opinions — and take advice! — from people who have no specialist knowledge in a field. The rule is simple: be careful who you take notice of because if you get the wrong information it will not help you succeed.

Routinely at Pola I saw women who were excellent consultants make business decisions on the advice of their husbands — and many of those men had no idea about business at all. The decisions were invariably bad.

Successful people have been a great source of information to me. Lionel Ward at the Wool Corporation was an encourager and supporter who taught me a great deal and gave me the confidence to ask questions. John Taylor at Pola taught me how to sell, build relationships with people and start thinking as a salesperson. They were what I call mentors, people who are prepared to guide you with their superior knowledge.

One of my favorite expressions is 'When the student is ready the teacher will appear'. And in my life this just happens every time. Whenever I'm thinking about what I need to do or become, someone comes along and helps me. I used to think this was complete coincidence and now I realise that when I put out those antennae signals that say 'This is what I need' I tend to get useful advice or help.

Often the people with the skills and knowledge are prepared to share their experience. I suppose it's a flattering role for them to become a mentor because another person is saying to you, 'Look, I admire you, could you help me become like you?' It's interesting that all my business mentors have been men, but not unexpected. After all, most of the top business seats are still occupied by men and it will be a good day, but a fair while, before that changes.

I can't imagine there will be a stage in my life where I won't need a mentor: there'll always be someone so much smarter, so much more able.

12
SECRET # 3
WORKING SMART

Good judgment comes from experience.
Experience comes from bad judgment.

written in my diary

As I made my first trip to Japan in 1982, a rival cosmetics company appeared on the horizon. It was an Australian company with a great marketing story: a local dermatologist had developed a skin-care product for Australian skin under the Australian sun. There was a million-dollar advertising campaign and a beautiful television ad. My advertising budget, of course, was zero. So how was I supposed to compete with this?

After seeing the TV ad for the umpteenth time, I decided to check out how the product was selling. The advertisements mentioned a nearby pharmacy as one stockist, so one morning on the way to work I dropped in.

I looked about but couldn't see the product, so I

asked the woman behind the counter. She looked puzzled.

'I don't think we sell that here.'

'But your pharmacy was one mentioned in the television advertisement as being a retailer.'

'I'm sorry, I don't know anything about it.'

I looked behind the counter. On the bottom shelf was the product.

'Look, I think that's it. Could you show me please?'

She had no idea it was there sitting on a shelf and she certainly had no training in the product. I don't know if this was an isolated case, but despite the expensive campaign and a great story, the product was dead within six months.

This was a lesson for me that a million-dollar advertising campaign didn't guarantee success; a lack of funds would be no excuse if I failed at Pola.

But there were other conclusions, too. The system of selling this product had failed where it most counted, with the customer. Despite a good product, a great deal of money and a lot of hard work, the planning did not work.

And the hard work wasn't good enough. It needed smart work: implementing and improving systems, seeking guidance from the best people, learning new skills. But smart work is about more than that. In smart work, the work must equal results. When I first started at Pola I had no title, no set role. It was a completely different world and a challenging time.

First, I had to learn about selling. I didn't really understand what selling was, so I had to learn the skills. Then I had to learn about what motivated people and how to get the best out of them. Sometimes I had to hold them by the hand and bring them along, and many dipped out. It was frustrating. I was so committed to making my life better, yet most people seemed so uncommitted, particularly when the word 'work' came up.

The pattern was hard work, a lot of focus and a lot of learning. My priorities were to recruit consultants and to sell product. It was a numbers game and it was easy to measure results. It didn't matter so much how many hours I worked, it was what I did to achieve the desired results. And the more accurately the results were measured the easier it was to determine future plans. It was a question of talking to a lot of people, persuading some of those people to join the company, persuading other people to at least try the product. And working smart to do so.

By 1994 Pola had a sophisticated training system in place. A new recruit, who I'll call Jane, seemed slow in getting off the mark. She'd paid several hundred dollars for her kit, attended three training sessions, watched the videos and read the sales manual from cover to cover. She had a reasonable knowledge of the different Pola lines available and the monthly specials that came and went. But she still hadn't held a presentation.

I quizzed her.

'Hello, Jane. I see you haven't made a presentation. Is there a problem?'

'No, nothing's wrong.'

'So, can I help you with something?'

'Well, I'm trying to learn everything in the manual.

There's so much. But when I know it all I'll be ready to hold a presentation.'

I couldn't believe it. She'd worked for dozens of hours but was nowhere near her first result. She needed to take action, make mistakes, test the plan. Yet all her work had produced nothing.

I know that if I'd needed to know everything about Pola before making my first presentation, I'd still be waiting to do it.

Like Jane, a lot of people work hard. They go to work every day, are always on time, always give their best. But at the end of their working life many of these people remain financially insecure or never achieve their dream. In Pola, many women worked long hours and achieved little; some worked fewer hours and made a great deal of money. So the solution isn't just hard work if you want to be successful, it's about smart work, thinking through what the possibilities are, and matching your talent and skills with the best possible outcome.

Every day there is so much to do, too much in fact. The key ingredient is to do the things that count, the ones that produce results for the total business. Deciding your priorities is fundamental. When I began Pola the goals were recruiting and sales. After John Taylor left, the focus became controlling costs and profit. Knowing what is most important and working on it is a key to success. And regularly reviewing those priorities is vital.

For me to work smart I have to ask myself: Do my actions fit my goals? How can I better reach my goals?

To do this it is essential to learn quickly from

mistakes. I found a lot of people at Pola kept doing the same things and wondered why they kept getting the same poor results. Everyone makes mistakes in business—I've made some big mistakes—but the key is to learn a fast lesson and be prepared to change direction. Smart people make fast learners—because one thing that particularly holds people back as entrepreneurs is the fear of making a mistake. What if I invest my money in this? What if I go down this track and it doesn't work? Well, if it doesn't work, just join the rest of the people out there risking their pride, their money, their self-esteem probably every day of the week to try something and give it a go.

I'm not suggesting you rush off into anything without making reasonable assessments and judgments, and getting opinions and advice from people who count—I certainly wouldn't—but beware advice from the wrong people as it can quickly put you down the wrong track. A lesson my friend Jane Jordan taught me: 'The quality of your life is related to the quality of your questions' was spot-on. If you ask a lot of questions and can distinguish between the answers, you're part-way there. And if you are dealing with people whose motives are not in your best interests, be careful.

In working smart you have to trust your own judgment. This doesn't mean flying by the seat of your pants and having fuzzy feelings about things. You must be able to assess the best way to go, then to have the courage to move down that path, while knowing that if you make a wrong choice you can always go back. Because judgment is based on something that has a valid base, gut feel, which relates to your experiences.

Gut feel saved my life in Austria when a girlfriend and I escaped a would-be attacker and his friends. By that stage of my travels I'd been all but attacked on a train in India and by a drunken mob of US soldiers in Thailand, so my gut-feel was strong.

As I built Pola I discovered it was terribly important not to put my life on hold. Many times I became completely exhausted and close to burning out, and it became clear that balance was essential. So I set rules about my work life, social life and health. Whenever those warning signs come up, it's generally a sign that I need to take a break, relax, exercise, get out of the office, walk in the park, reinvigorate. Of course it's not always possible to do this immediately, but I'm conscious that exhaustion reduces my effectiveness. I've also made my worst business decisions when I was exhausted.

Balance is the key and each year I address the other parts of my life with the same enthusiasm as I address business, revising my goals, finding new ways to improve things.

If all you have is business, problems get out of proportion, your patience with people declines, you get bored, burned out, frustrated. A bigger picture is essential. How many people burn out on the way to success? They make it to the 'If only' brigade. If only they'd had a better sense of humour, more balance, they might have made it.

Working smart means being open to new ideas, always being willing to learn.

In the first years at Pola I listened to a lot of speakers, on stage, in seminars, on tape, and started tapping into a whole new level of energy—because I had never heard motivational speakers, I didn't know what they were about. I'd never read books on selling or attitude or anything like that, and I started to voraciously consume that information by reading books, just tapping into a new level of energy.

Today I still go to seminars and read books to learn new ideas, new ways of doing things. Because smart work is about being aware of what tools are available to do the job.

I'm fascinated by the concept of lateral thinking, brainstorming and coming in from different angles to solve problems. I think one of the things that makes you successful in business is how creatively you can attack problems and develop new realities, new paradigms, instead of looking at things the same old way and thinking the same old way. Some businesses get stuck in a rut and die. If a business is not open to new ideas it can be disastrous for that business.

Working smart means developing two other skills required for success: commitment and discipline.

13

SECRET # 4 CONSISTENT PERSISTENT EFFORT

*Nothing in the world can take the place of persistence.
Talent will not; nothing is more common than
unsuccessful men with talent.
Genius will not; unrewarded genius is almost a proverb.
Education will not; the world is full of
educated derelicts.
Persistence and determination alone are omnipotent.*

Calvin Coolidge, US President 1923–29

It's often hard to get out of bed in the morning for a five kilometre run, particularly in winter when it's raining, windy and cold. It's worse when I wake up 20 minutes before my jogging time and lie there. At the end of the 20 minutes I have talked myself out of getting out of bed: it's too cold, you've done six days in a row, have a break — the easiest thing is to find a reason not to get up. The only way I can avoid this

CONSISTENT PERSISTENT EFFORT

negativity is to be woken by the alarm; I just simply jump out of bed without thinking.

It's fascinating, the self-talk undermining an activity that I enjoy, know is beneficial, and reinvigorates me.

But every morning I have to really motivate myself as I'm jogging and the only way I can do that is to think how I am going to look if I give up exercise, how people do look when they don't exercise. They look overweight, unhappy, they look sloppy. I use all these words to try and motivate myself to get out and go jogging. Every morning I put myself to the test. Every morning I search for that commitment to myself. I don't pass the test every morning. I don't go running every morning, but I pass the test most of the time, probably suffice to say that I pass the test about six times a week on average.

This commitment — a consistent, persistent effort — is essential in my personal and business lives. Pola would not have developed without persistence — the continual telephoning, meetings, presentations, recruitments, rejections. It was a source of energy that was inspired not only by my dream of building a company but by the fear of failing.

This source of energy comes from the belief in the possibility of a dream — I call it the opportunity of the big picture.

To build a business there is a simple formula: long hours, hard (smart) work and a good product. It is common to almost everyone who has built a business. This is a basic ingredient that could be taught in any business school. It is so simple — but it is not easy.

Commitment to goals is essential to success. The only formula I know for keeping commitment burning is to revisit the goals and dreams and to get excited about how your life will look when you achieve those things: to believe them, feel them, see them, touch them. Like when I lie in bed on a cold morning picturing myself as an unhealthy, unfit, unhappy person.

One big drawback with direct selling is that it costs so little to get involved that it attracts all sorts of people. They may have good intentions, but whether they have the courage or character to pursue something is another question. A lot go into direct selling, but few follow it through to great success and prosper.

If, for example, you buy a McDonald's franchise it may cost $1 million. This produces seriously committed people, people who really want to make a go of their business. But when it only costs a few hundred dollars to get involved, you get a mixed level of commitment. In some ways it is too easy to join: if there was a threshold of $10,000 or $20,000, the level of commitment would be quite different.

Yet low-cost entry is one of its strengths, paradoxically. You can start a small business on very little, which is what I was able to do when I was broke in 1982. But while some who join are committed, most just give it a go and see what happens. And if you wait and see what happens in life, absolutely nothing happens—unless you make it happen.

CONSISTENT PERSISTENT EFFORT

I got very frustrated dealing with a lot of people to find that small percentage who were prepared to make a consistent, persistent effort. But the few were worth the frustration; you could measure it in their incomes and enjoy it in the strength and vitality of their company. Equally frustrating were people who weren't prepared to take responsibility for themselves. Perhaps much of this related to women's expectations and their upbringings — they could marry and rely on a male breadwinner, taking a passive financial and economic role. That was my upbringing, partly my expectation. It didn't pan out that way and I had to develop another strategy to survive.

When I started with Pola I had a passionate guiding force that kept me working through obstacle after obstacle and negativity after negativity: I wanted my security and independence.

There were two ways for me to do that. One, I could have married a wealthy man — and I may do that if I fall in love with one who has the right qualities. The other was to get up and get going myself. This incredible passion to become less dependent on other people, to take responsibility, to look after myself, became the commitment that kept me going. I had extraordinary doubts but I had this really powerful driving force and that gave me extraordinary focus on what I was doing.

Clarity truly is power. When you have clarity about what you want, it gives you the strength and courage to achieve it. And that's what commitment's about. It's about having the day-in day-out commitment to the achievement of that goal.

Whether it's business or emotional life, once you have commitment about your goals you have to keep putting in daily, consistent, persistent effort.

I have favorite sayings and expressions I use to inspire and remotivate myself. Many I write in the front of my business diary, so each day when I look forward to what's coming up I can get an extra boost. I don't know *how* it happens, just that *it works*.

One of my favorite expressions is about habits: 'For the first 20 years of your life you make your habits, and then your habits make you.'

In my childhood — and I think a lot about the habits of discipline instilled by my parents and the nuns at the school — discipline was one of the deepest lessons I was given continually throughout my childhood and adolescence. And as much as sometimes I wanted to resist that, I realise now that the habit of discipline is one of the most valuable habits you can have, because it's not something you have to think about.

I notice a lot of people have no sense of discipline. They are diverted continuously from whatever they set out to do. They don't have the discipline to say no or get on with the job. I really practice at being disciplined. Even to this day I haven't just got that habit, I still have to work at it. Discipline isn't just there. Getting out of bed for the morning run can be hard. Being tempted by the wrong foods requires restraint. It's an ongoing challenge.

CONSISTENT PERSISTENT EFFORT

People say, 'You're a very disciplined person.' Really they should say 'You really work at being disciplined.'

And one way I do that is through my morning run. I feel it is my way of reassuring myself that I still have the habit of discipline.

Not having discipline can lead people down all sorts of tracks where all of a sudden it's all totally out of hand, whether it's the consumption of alcohol or drugs, or just losing balance and going overboard in any particular direction. It seems that indiscipline starts off in small ways and builds up and eats at you over the years so that in the end you become incapable of making decisions about discipline.

Once you get older, habits are harder to change, but it is still possible. I've worked hard to develop habits that are beneficial to my health, my body and my mind. I grew up on country cooking — roasts, pavlovas, cream cakes — but now have developed the habit of eating salads, fruits and healthy meals. It's become so routine I don't think of fatty or sweet foods. And if I do, I wonder what I would look like if I ate enough of them. That soon reminds me of why I have a healthy diet. And I know people (and about others) whose lives were messes, dire messes, who have forced disciplined regimens on themselves and won through.

As I run along the river every morning around 6.30am I do a lot of creative thinking, refocus myself. I'm exercising, getting fresh air, noticing the environment around me. In winter I often see the stars and the moon, and the sun coming up with the moon not yet down, always so spectacular. No matter what goes

HIGH-HEELED SUCCESS

on in business later that day or the frustrations I might have to deal with, I've got that memory of me being out early in the morning watching the sun rise, running along a river, watching people row.

And work isn't happy and joyful every day. There are some tasks at work you really hate to do but without discipline you'll never do them, you won't succeed in your business. Every athlete, Olympic champion knows the value of discipline, and yet really life is just like one long Olympic Games without a break. Just surviving, keeping your head above water. When Prime Minister Malcolm Fraser said 'Life's not meant to be easy', he was very possibly right. I don't know whether it was *meant* to be easy or not, but it's *not* easy. And without a lot of discipline you just don't make it. It gets on top of you, it gets you down. Discipline for me is like a key element for my being able to cope, survive and particularly deal with life on my own because at times life on your own is so hard, so tough, so lonely, that without self-discipline, you just won't make it.

Sometimes you just don't want to get out of bed in the morning: it's too lonely out there, too hard, too tough, people are demanding too much of you, you'd just rather cop out. Discipline alone enables you to keep going.

Your habits determine whether or not you make it every day, and make it towards the end you have in mind.

14

SECRET # 5
SSSHHH!

Have courage, life is short

written in my diary

A few years ago I spent two weeks in one of my favorite places in the world, Aspen, Colorado. I was enjoying myself so much that on the final day I took the last possible flight to Denver and connection to New York.

I arrived in New York very late. There were no taxis available so I took a bus into the Port Authority bus station at West 33rd Street. As I struggled with my two suitcases — carrying them alternately because they were too heavy to carry simultaneously — a passenger offered to help, saying it was not the time or place for a woman to be on her own. He helped me to a taxi that dropped me at a small hotel at 54th and Madison.

Only after the taxi drove off I realised the hotel was locked and I was alone on the streets of Manhattan at 2am. I started banging on the windows and finally woke the night porter who took me to my room. As grateful as I was to be off the streets, the room looked to my Australian eyes like an inside-out prison cell. All the locks were on the inside. My Rocky Mountain high was beginning to subside. I bolted my room door shut and fell asleep.

Next morning around 10 o'clock I went walking down Madison Avenue. As I wandered along in a dream, two very large men came up beside me, one on each side like bodyguards, and started walking in step with me.

Because of my Aspen state of mind I did not have my normal wary traveller guard up, like wearing my handbag under my coat. Instead, my shoulder bag was outside my jacket. Suddenly it felt much lighter. I looked down to see the flap open and my wallet gone. The two men were still on either side of me.

I kept walking and looked from one to the other, realising that one of them had my wallet. I turned to the man closest to my bag and said, 'Excuse me, I have just lost my wallet. I am an Australian travelling alone and my wallet contains everything I need — my passport, credit cards, airline ticket and money.' The man looked at me and handed me back my wallet! I thanked him and the two walked off.

A woman, a New Yorker, came up and told me she had seen everything from behind. She was even more stunned than I was that the man had given it back to me. She left and I stood alone, shaking, in the street. To this day I am unsure what exactly made him do it — my Australian accent? the sheer honesty of my request? the calm and polite way I asked for the wallet? — but I'm sure thinking positively helped. It had the power to make a thief give up on this theft.

Thinking positively

Attitude is how you look at things. What you say, what you think, what you do. And the most important factor is to be positive, even when things go wrong — or your wallet disappears!

A lot of people dismiss positive thinking as American hype. I disagree. The thinking it encourages is to make one more conscious, more in control, more responsible.

Everyone is at some time affected by problems, disasters, mistakes. The question is how you react to these incidents. If you cave in to the problems around you, you've really lost it. At many times in my life when I've had significant problems I've had to just really work through them knowing that unless I do life is just going to be a downward trek.

If you seek to blame — as I blamed my husband for some time after we went broke — you get nowhere. If you seek to solve the problem, put it behind you and get on, then you will progress. As the saying goes, 'You are allowed to look back at the past but you are not allowed to stare.'

Many women I worked with said their attitude was part of them. 'That's the way I am,' they'd say. 'That's me.' They're not willing to change their attitude, take control of what they think, what they do — and how they react to adversity.

When would-be consultants failed to turn up, I had to stay positive. No point saying, 'Woe is me'. I was responsible. I had to say to myself, 'It wasn't her fault she didn't get to the meeting. It was mine.'

And looking at it that way I thought, 'What am I doing here? How do I stop this happening again? Why don't I tighten up the system?' So I put in a new system: before travelling long distances I required would-be consultants to make a commitment: either invest money in advance or organise a presentation and provide me with the names of at least 10 people who would be there. And this worked; sometimes the organiser of the presentation wasn't really interested but I found an ideal consultant in the audience.

There is no alternative to thinking positively when things go wrong. Sometimes it's hard to see *anything* positive. But the option is too horrific. Despair and unhappiness.

When I worked at the Wool Corporation I knew Roland Perry, who had worked in the public relations department. In 1990 we bumped into each other and caught up for dinner. Roland said he was looking for a place to live. I had a spare bedroom in the flat and was short of cash. I hadn't shared for a long time. After thinking about it for a while, we negotiated a rent and Roland moved in.

He'd been there about three weeks when he said, 'I want to do an article on you.'

I'd had no media exposure at this stage and was quite unsure. I'd never opened up about my life, my business.

'What sort of article?'

'On your achievements. A woman from nothing achieving something.'

And he said he wanted to do a story on another woman in parallel.

'What sort of story?'

'Two stories of success.'

We had a long discussion because I didn't want to go into my personal life. And so we set aside some time and taped an interview for the article.

I went skiing and the day before the article came out I saw a promotion: Next to a picture of me was the headline,

RICH WOMAN, POOR WOMAN

I knew which one I was going to be. I felt sick. I knew 24 hours ahead this was going to be a nightmare.

Next day I went fearfully to the newsagent to get the *Sunday Age*. On page three of the supplement there was a picture of me on a sofa next to a picture of a woman behind an ironing board in a Ministry of Housing home.

The headline read:

BOTH THESE WOMEN ARE INTELLIGENT AND
SUCCESSFUL
YET ONE ENDED UP IN THE PENTHOUSE
AND ONE IN THE POORHOUSE
WHY?

I was speechless. For a start, my small flat was no penthouse. The full-page article was worse. It started:

Marcia Griffin is one of Australia's most successful women . . . She owns property in South Yarra, lives in a comfortable apartment overlooking the Royal Botanic Gardens with views of the city and drives a white Holden Integra.

Ms Griffin has regular trips to other states and abroad, including skiing holidays in Aspen, Colorado. For relaxation she gives dinner parties. Her friends, her guests, are often rich and famous. In recent months her guests have included [and he named a top businessman, a famous stockbroker and his wife, a former Miss Australia, an actress, a socialite, a top lawyer, prominent gays, a black American basketballer and a novelist]. She loves eating out and her favourite restaurant is Fannys.

Ms Griffin, who is in her 40s, would not disclose her income, but rival company executives say it would be between $130,000 and $160,000 a year, depending on bonuses.

Fitness is important to her. She runs around the Botanic Garden's Tan track. She is a good social tennis player and the Lindsay Fox Wimbledon-size trophy — which she won in doubles with the millionaire businessman in a private tournament — sits proudly in her home study. On cold weekend afternoons lately she has been learning to sail.

At 40, Barbara Dixon's main occupation is looking after her 15-year-old daughter Deanna, who had Down's syndrome and the mental age of between four and eight.

The years of struggle have been etched into her face but she has not lost a sense of humour that has been sharpened rather than dulled by her experiences.

Ms Dixon has a pension that brings in about $9000 a year. She lives in a neat immaculately kept Ministry of Housing home in Bonbeach, has no car and uses public transport.

She is a 40-a-day smoker and cannot go out in the sun because of a medical condition (*Lupus*) . . .

The article went on to say how Barbara Dixon had been bullied as a child, had shock treatment as a teenager after being admitted to a psychiatric hospital, was diagnosed with an auto-immune disease that affected her facial skin, married, had a handicapped child, divorced her soldier husband and went on the pension.

I was painted as having a fabulous education, travelling the world, studying at university and dropping law 'because it was boring', marrying a barrister and getting a new job that allowed me to travel over more of the world. A rich, showy boastful woman. It sounded like I said to the journalist, 'Here, come and look at my Lindsay Fox tournament trophy. And guess who came to dinner last week? Guess who my friends are?'

Quite a few people were mentioned by name — and I've taken their names from the article to respect their privacy — because Roland Perry had heard me speak to them on the telephone or they had come to dinner while he was staying. He'd written about things in my apartment that few people knew about. I quickly got on the phone and rang those people named to apologise. They were very good about it: they knew Roland was sharing my apartment and worked out what had happened.

I felt I never wanted to return to Melbourne. Each time I read the article it looked worse. I could see nothing positive about it. I looked so boastful, disgraceful and upwardly mobile. It was completely humiliating.

A week later I drove back to Melbourne knowing Roland had to go. I could no longer live in the same building as him. I arrived late and Roland opened the door. I could barely look at him, I was still so upset.

'Great article, wasn't it?'

I paused.

'I think it's one of the worst things that's ever happened to me. I've been sick all week.'

And then he said something to me that I never lost the point of: 'Well, if that's the way you respond to publicity, you're not going to make it. If you want to have a profile and you're going to react like that you'll never make it.'

And, as angry as I was with him, I did absorb what he was saying. After all, he *knew* this media and PR world; I did not. Then I asked him to leave, which he did the next day.

It was hard for me to think positively about the article but the next day the phone rang and rang and rang. And I realised the power of the media. Calls ranged from an invitation to go on a board to people wanting to join Pola.

And once the phone began to ring I realised the article had put Pola on the map. I don't know about Ms Dixon's reaction; I didn't have the strength to call her to find out. All I know was that while Roland Perry upset me, he'd also taught me that the media was an incredible way to get publicity, especially when I had no advertising budget. I just had to shift my attitude and take control, as much as I could, about what I said and who I spoke to. Over the following years Pola received an enormous amount of publicity which was wonderful for the business.

Being Positive

Keeping a positive attitude also means keeping yourself in top condition; the links between physical and mental health and performance have been well documented. If I'm physically or mentally run down, it's so much harder to be positive when things go wrong.

My success has been greatly helped by the fact I've been fit and healthy, both of which I work on daily. I exercise, eat good foods, drink little alcohol, don't smoke, don't abuse my body.

I think we all need some sort of recourse to fall back on and the other thing I fall back on is my healthy life, because even when I'm depressed or unhappy about something, I always feel grateful that I'm healthy. Essentially, this drives me to lead a healthy life because I know that when all else fails, your health is that basic thing that carries you through.

I strongly believe in the importance of appearance, that it is a reflection of how you see yourself. How I think about myself reflects in how I look and how I feel, and if I don't think good things of myself I won't treat myself well. The expression, 'Your body is a temple not an amusement parlor' needs wider currency: you should treat the body as a temple and I really do treat mine like a sacred building. Every now and again when I drink too much wine I feel disgusted with myself next morning because I feel dreadful. I look in the mirror and see blood-shot eyes. But most importantly I'm upset because I have treated my body badly because it responds violently to too much alcohol.

Part of my concern about my appearance comes from fear of losing control over my body shape, letting go, not looking my best. I see that happen to people and it's normally triggered by a crisis.

When I turned 40 I began to notice lines were forming around my mouth and eyes. Despite a good skin-care routine, I was starting to look old.

The answer? Cosmetic surgery.

In America I'd met many older women who looked fantastic. Women in their 50s looked as if they were in their late 30s. Those in their 40s looked as if they were in their early 30s. I became interested and began researching what cosmetic surgery would mean, speaking to surgeons, friends and women who'd had it done.

I was terrified by the idea. Apart from a few days when I lost my baby, I'd never spent time in hospital. Why would I possibly volunteer to become sick? What about the pain? And what if it went wrong and I was left scarred? How would the head of a cosmetics company look with a damaged face? Friends gave me no encouragement; in fact they were all negative when I raised the topic. And I faced the strong influence of my Catholic upbringing: What gave me the right to interfere with God's work? Would God punish me?

It took a couple of years before I could confront my fears and summon up the courage to do something about the ever-deepening lines. I didn't feel the surgery was going to change my life or solve any problems — I wanted it because it was available.

My surgeon said, 'If you're not ready for it you shouldn't do it. Your life is already fabulous. This is just cream on the cake.'

And that was the way I felt about it. On the spur of the moment I gave the surgeon a cheque for $1000 as a deposit. Nothing like money to commit you to a project.

In late 1994 I went into hospital for the operation. I was still scared, and certainly out of my comfort zone, but I'd dug deep and somehow found the courage. A hospital was not a place I wanted to spend time in. But I knew I wanted this done.

I woke with my face bandaged and, for a few moments, thought something had gone horribly wrong and I was blind. As I slowly recovered I was amazed there was no pain. On day four, I summoned up the courage to look in the mirror and was relieved to see less bruising than I expected. The surgeon said it had all gone well. And that proved to be the case. Each day the swelling went down and my bruising cleared up. I spent 12 days in hospital, reading, sleeping, eating and being looked after by a professional, understanding medical staff. It was like a holiday, a relief from the pressure I'd built up on myself. And, when it came time to leave, I burst into tears. I cried uncontrollably for more than an hour and a half, letting go those emotions that had built up. I'd conquered my worst fears — surgery and hospitals. It was very therapeutic because when I'd cried myself dry, that was it. It was over.

My next challenge was to go back into the real world and, at first, I was scared to leave my house, so each day I'd drive my car just a little further: first to the end of the street, then around the block, then to the local shops.

Only 21 days after surgery I went to a drinks party feeling very self-conscious. No need; people told me how relaxed I looked and asked if I'd been on holiday. Then I went to see my family in the country. I was sure they would notice, but they didn't. They just told me how well I looked.

The outcome was fantastic and I wouldn't hesitate to have cosmetic surgery again if I wanted it. Most women spend a lot of money on their appearance, from clothes to cosmetics, in a bid to look their best. And while cosmetic surgery is expensive, it is just another option. I saved money for more than a year before my operation. My attitude is that if you don't want your face to look lined or older, why not take advantage of whatever possibilities there are?

In the same way your personal appearance can affect how people see you, the appearance of a business can also leave an instant impression.

At Pola, I'd sometimes hear the tone of our receptionist's voice and think it was just not right; or friends would tell me she sounded unfriendly. And nothing used to make me crosser than someone ringing into Pola and wanting a product or wanting to join the company and getting a hostile, bored or surly voice.

So often in organisations we overlook the simple things, and the first contact counts a lot. These are critical things, not little things. How's the attitude in your front office?

When I walk into a hotel I believe I can tell what sort of general manager runs the business. Recently I walked into a big hotel in Brisbane and received a deathly greeting. The staff looked across and continued doing something terribly important and here I was, the customer, about to spend hundreds of dollars, being ignored. What did that say for the energy, focus and attitude of the business?

I know when times get tough I always find something to console me in nature. Lying in bed listening to the rain reminds me of my childhood and the importance of rain in the country. Whatever obstacle comes along I always feel at least there's the stars, the sky, the moon, the sun — and the simple things on the planet that are so beautiful and incredibly sustaining.

I can walk from my home to the river, sit and look at the water. I find it refreshing to take solace in nature. It helps put matters in perspective and refresh the spirit.

And the human spirit is so much part of who we are, part of our attitude, our creativity, our energy, our drive. It is vital we protect it.

Comedian Richard Stubbs recently rejected a reported $1.5 million salary to host a national breakfast radio show. Why? He said: 'If you see your creativity as a resource, then I think you have to protect it and not just red-line it constantly. You have to recognise it can run out, that you can burn yourself out, and you need to take time to sit back and relax a bit and let the creativity work again.'

Former Prime Minister Paul Keating put it this way: 'You have to feed the inner existence, the inner life, so I try to do that. Not as an objective but just simply as something you need to do. And I think that's what gives you some of the zest and ability to keep looking forward.'

Protection can come in the form of walking down to the river, the beach or the park, or taking time out on a holiday. Whatever you do, ensure you protect your spirit. It is who you are.

Your thoughts can be influenced by who you mix with. If you spend time with negative people, chances are you'll pick up negative influences. Avoid them.

I find it wise to keep my own counsel, by which I mean I don't throw around my thoughts for general consumption. I don't ask people, 'What do you think I should do?' I seek only selected people, mentors, and ask them. I'm careful who I take advice from.

Improving

Every time I get into too much of a pattern, too much of a routine, I find myself being pulled down. I hate the feeling that life's not going to change much and everything's pretty much the same, so I work hard to avoid it. It's important to me that I'm seeking new challenges.

I adopt new ideas, set new goals, try new systems, all to improve either my personal life or my business. I find myself constantly seeking and embracing change, and renewing my energy and yet maintaining my deepest values.

And in today's business world change is a massive issue, especially in communications, media and computers. Unless you are constantly being made aware of developments and adapting your thinking, it is easy to get left behind in business.

I probably knew more when I was 20 than I know now. Maybe it's the wealth of knowledge in the world growing so rapidly, technology changing so rapidly. Just as I think I know about something, I hear there's something else that's new. And to work with people of different generations is a great asset because they are tuning into different areas of technology and life.

I find this enlivening. Each day I learn something new and feel differently about things than I did previously. I feel like each day is the petal of a flower opening up — there's something fascinating and new out there and I have to grasp it in order to take the next step in life and in business.

For some people this is very uncomfortable because when you can settle into your comfort zone you don't have to change — for a lot of people that seems an easier way to go. In business, some people and some companies slide into a zone where nothing happens, little changes and the business slides slowly into disrepair or is swept away by the first storm or change it hits. No one is really interested in what's happening.

Nowadays, at least, I find my comfort zone an *un*comfortable place. I prefer to be continually making small changes in my life rather than getting into some sleepy tired hollow and being rocked out of it by the reality of circumstances around me.

Laughing

Not long after winning the Businesswoman of the Year Award I was asked to fly to Chicago to give the closing address at a prestigious seminar. The speaker line-up was unbelievable and the opportunity a one-off. I was very excited.

I worked hard writing and rewriting my talk. I wanted to illustrate it with overhead slides and organised for pictures of various aspects of Pola, a map transposing Australia on to the United States to show the similar sizes of the country — I even drove to the country and took pictures of where I grew up, including the tiny school at Wickliffe, 240 kilometres from Melbourne.

When I arrived in Chicago I was met by a public relations consultant, Bob. After settling into the hotel, he took me to the seminar and introduced me to the audio-visual team. The auditorium was large and on each side of the stage were huge screens. There was a remote control button for the slides, which the audio-visual man told me to press once.

'Once you've done that you don't have to worry again. We'll do the rest.'

'But how will you know which slide I'll be talking about?'

'Don't worry, we've been doing this for years. We know exactly. We'll be listening for the cues and we'll know what to do.'

They were insistent. All I had to do was press the button for the first slide and they'd do the rest.

Bob chipped in with some advice. 'Marcia, it looks much better if you don't turn to the side and look at the slides. Just talk about them but don't turn around and look at them.'

This seemed good advice so when I stood up as the last speaker at the seminar I began my talk and pressed the button for the first slide, the picture I'd taken weeks earlier of Wickliffe State School Number 948, where it all began for me. My speech lasted 45 minutes and I got a great ovation — I felt I'd done a really good job.

Bob came up, beaming. 'Great talk, but what happened to the slides?'

'I'm sorry, what do you mean, "What happened to the slides?"?'

'Well, after the school we didn't see anything else.'

I couldn't believe it. I had gone through this whole speech for 45 minutes, I had 16 fantastic slides that cost more than $1000 to prepare and only one had come up. I'd had three rehearsals with the audio-visual man but he hadn't changed a slide. And the whole time I'd been talking to pictures I thought were on the screen.

I whipped down the back of the room to see the

audio-visual people but they'd disappeared. To this day I have no idea what happened or why it didn't work. I was shattered.

But that night I went to dinner with Bob and laughed a lot, especially about the fact I was so confident that I was speaking to the perfect picture on the screen.

Being able to laugh at myself is something that's very important. Looking back at Roland Perry's interview and how pompous I appeared makes me laugh today.

I think I picked up a habit of laughing at myself and laughing at the ridiculous in my early 20s when I travelled. I remember jumping out of a car in Spain when the male driver put his hand up my friend's skirt. We demanded he stop and as I jumped out I pulled my suitcase from the car. It fell to the ground but I still clutched the handle. The irate driver sped off and we stood on the edge of the road in the middle of nowhere, looking at my suitcase and the separated handle, in fits of laughter.

In being positive it also helps keep things in perspective. Some people just lose all idea of what's important. I know people who always need something bigger, faster, brighter — it's the most important thing to them. At a party before Christmas I met a woman who was distressed because her cleaning lady had broken her hand. The woman was so upset — not for the cleaning lady — but because the dirty house would ruin her summer holiday . . .

Each morning I wake up and think how lucky I am to live in Australia. Despite our problems, there's no wars, famines or epidemics of disease that ravage other countries. I deeply appreciate where I live.

And finally, when things go well, give yourself a pat on the back. Celebrate. Do something crazy. Break the rules. Party. Because to keep the spirit alive you have to keep the child inside you alive, to be excited, open to new ideas and full of dreams.

Book Four

Six Facts of Life

People don't grow old. When they stop
  growing, they become old.

It's easy to avoid criticism:
Say nothing, do nothing, be nothing

Men are from Detroit,
Women are from Paris

15

WOMEN'S BUSINESS

Sugar and spice and all things passionate and athletic and creative and soft and wild and fun and intelligent and strong and tender and wonderful — that's what little girls are made of

written in my diary

When I became a teacher in the late 1960s the government paid me 10 per cent less than men with the same qualifications. Bank loans were all but impossible for single women to get. For single men? No problem. We were devalued, blocked in our opportunities.

All this seems alien now.

In the 1970s, 1980s and 1990s many structural barriers and male psychological prejudices have been shattered, holed or badly damaged. The feminists have done women a great service and women have made huge progress in the workforce. The bad news is that some barriers remain intact and probably will for a long time to come.

Yet the bottom line is that opportunities have never been better for women. After hundreds of years staying home, cooking and looking after children, women are out there in the tough world of business. There have never been so many open doors.

So why aren't we succeeding?

Well, we are, but not enough of us, and not as thoroughly as we could.

Up until 1982 I worked with a mix of men and women. From 1982 on, at Pola, I worked almost exclusively with women, thousands and thousands of them from all walks of life. I continually came across common themes that partly explained why so few women succeeded and why so many failed.

Instinct

Men in business have a preparedness to go into the unknown, to take risks: I guess they just have something that is more instinctively entrepreneurial than women. It seems women who become entrepreneurs — people who make something of value from nothing — sometimes do it by chance. Men have a more focused entrepreneurial approach. Perhaps that's just the experience men have from hundreds of years of being in business and passing that information on to each other, encouraging each other and supporting each other. It is interesting to speculate on why this is so, but the main thing is that it *is* so.

Most women are risk-averse, instinctively frightened of taking the risks needed in business, even in direct selling where the risk level is very low indeed. Women would rather spend a few hundred dollars on a new pair of shoes than put that investment in a business.

I don't pretend I'm immune. My biggest mistake in my 15 years at Pola was not to buy the business when I was offered the chance by the Japanese in 1987. To me, the risk was too high. I had only just begun to get back on my feet financially and was not prepared to chance everything on a company that was losing money when I took it over. A couple of years later I would have jumped at the chance, but the offer was not made a second time. Instead, the company profits stayed in the company. I did earn a small stake in the company based on its sales growth and so shared in the profits, but the rewards were tiny compared with the opportunity I'd knocked back. It was a lesson I learned the hard way; you have to take risks to get ahead. And I often see women who, like I was in 1987, are not prepared to take a risk on something that could produce great rewards.

Until women really change their attitude they are always going to be the people in jobs, working for someone else, usually a man. And that man will always be getting greater financial independence and security because of that very attitude to risk-taking and entrepreneurship.

Being tough-minded

You have to be tough minded in business, be able to show strong character. It's a huge advantage being firm in your mental attitude, being very convinced about following the things you believe in.

But a lot of women see tough-mindedness as making them the butt of jokes about aggressive, masculine women, jokes that will alienate them from men. This factor no doubt holds Australian women back — in America it's different. The attitude of some Australian men towards successful women is very negative. I've encountered this quite a few times, and for the most part it makes me laugh. And success is the best revenge. Those who laughed at me when I went door to door with a cardboard box of cosmetics didn't laugh when it turned into a multi-million-dollar business. Success is a sweet non-aggressive revenge. Most businessmen I know, however, have been very supportive. They aren't threatened by the success of a female; they're tough minded and pragmatic; therefore, they're free.

Emotions

Another great male strength is the ability to separate their emotional life from their business life. Men can put things in boxes and say, 'This is business', 'This is home life'. They can be instinctive and tough-minded at work and leave it there. But many women interlink the two, unable to put things in those two boxes. A lot of women take their personal lives to work with them, worrying about their home life, their children, their relationships, their feelings. And women often talk about their feelings, including 'I don't feel like doing it today'. Men just submerge their feelings and do it. Maybe it's something in our genes, the instincts of motherhood and home-making, that makes us less able to put things into boxes. What I do know is that it affects and limits a lot of women in their work life.

Though I have no children, I still sometimes find it pretty hard to distinguish my emotional and business life, and so I well understand women who have this problem. Yet I see men go through shocking personal problems — a mid-life crisis, emotional break-ups, business troubles, divorce — but they seem to just keep going at work, getting on with business. And their business benefits. Because if you don't have that discipline to keep emotional and business life separate, your business will suffer.

So often feminists ignore these distinctions and pretend they don't exist. They just talk about the structural limits. It would be better if feminists addressed the things that really held women back — and not just the glass ceilings imposed by men. Yet it seems almost politically incorrect to say that women are holding themselves back.

I have met such a tiny number of women who have been able to stay completely focused on their work despite events going on in their emotional lives. Those that have made it in business have been extraordinarily independent and strong in character.

I would like to think all women have the same opportunity as men to succeed — and that doesn't mean just having the same education or the same job opportunities. In part it means thinking the way men think about business, because often men's thinking is what leads them to greater success. What you think is what you are.

And I've seen so many women thrown off track because they were influenced by external factors. If you see business and emotions as interconnected it's going to be pretty hard to be focused on business, because there are always going to be issues that impinge on it.

Fear

My greatest frustration while running Pola was watching helplessly as women with huge potential — fabulous personalities, great relaters to people, those who could be a big success in selling — did not succeed because of fear. Fear of success, fear of losing the man in their life, fear of alienating themselves from their friends, fear of being on their own if they became too successful.

And this was not helped by many men.

In Japan, partners do not become involved in business. In Western culture it's quite the opposite and it's unlikely to change. Involving partners has benefits, but so many times I saw the negative side, women dragged down by the opinions or actions or advice of their partners.

And when the men got involved in any way, shape or form, the influence was usually very negative. They often had the attitude of 'I know better' or 'This is smarter'.

And these women took their men's advice. They allowed men to make decisions about things that the men were not experts in or knew nothing about. So often I came across great women in relationships with men who were not very financially successful or financially capable, but these women took the advice of these men instead of saying, 'Look, you're the person I want to be emotionally involved with but it doesn't necessarily mean I should trust your business judgments. I will trust my own.'

It is a fascinating contrast to me that there are many men who go out, work hard, achieve, build businesses, yet their wives hardly know what they do. Those men can separate their business and emotional lives very successfully.

A key personal aim at Pola was to encourage women to become independent, to make their own business decisions. That didn't mean they couldn't be in an emotional relationship — far from it. They just had to separate business and emotions.

One of the great problems for women is learning to trust their own judgments and learning to get opinions from the men and women who really count — people who have really succeeded, not people with whom women may have an emotional relationship.

I've made plenty of mistakes in this area and it took me a long time to trust my own judgment and distinguish between emotion and business. My husband was a top barrister but had little idea about money management and we ended up broke. I've taken business advice from men because I may have had an emotional attachment, and equally those ideas weren't very good and I lost money as a result.

Support

When I won the Businesswoman of the Year Award well over half the congratulatory messages, calls and notes were from men, which I found fascinating. My business was based on supporting women and there were thousands working at Pola, yet even among my team there were some who were not congratulatory.

I think one's ability to be genuinely enthusiastic about the success of other people is directly related to one's own inner feelings of how successful one can be if one really wants to be. And if you feel you have that ability to be as successful as you want to be, then you are happy to see other people succeed. But if you have genuine fear about your own ability, then I think you are going to be restrained in praise by jealousy. That's how I see a lot of women behave towards each other. Superficially, they can appear to be supportive, but deep down they don't have a sufficient sense of security about their own purpose and direction to really congratulate other women.

And it doesn't matter how much feminists talk about supporting each other and networking with each other, it's painfully obvious to me when I go to functions where there are a lot of women, that only a small percentage have genuine feelings of self-confidence and therefore the genuine ability to praise other women, support other women, to be genuinely congratulatory towards other women. I think at this point in the evolution of women in business there are far too many insecure women to be genuinely supportive of each other. I know a lot of women will not want to hear that, but that's my deepest belief.

When women start thinking more like men they will become more supportive of each other, because for as long as women feel insecure about their lives, their futures and their financial security I don't believe they are capable of supporting each other.

Sadly, I also came across a lot of men who gave their partners little support — they just wanted the woman at home looking after him while he got on with his career, and the pressure put on the woman was something she took to work. If you employ people it is a good idea to work out who the woman is with, what her husband's attitudes are and whether he'll be supportive of her putting extra effort in the business. Because I have seen women pulled down in an organisation because they are under pressure from a man at home, saying 'Why aren't you home? Why isn't dinner on the table?'

Changing the Rules?

Many years ago, when I was working at the Australian Wool Corp, I did a brief course called 'Women in Management', and I've never forgotten what the lecturer Ruth Wisniak said:

'When women get a really good job everyone says, "Isn't that great?" When men get a really good job everyone says, "Where do you go after that?"'

It was so true. I had a great job and everyone said to me, 'You've got a really good job. Isn't that great?' Sure, I had a good job. But no one asked me — and I kept thinking to myself — where do I go from here?

As a child I remember boys being asked 'What do you want to be when you grow up?' The girls weren't asked. At university, the boys had their fathers as role models: bankers, doctors, businessmen. At my girls' school, even though we were encouraged to go to university and expand our minds, it was almost accepted that we would go on, marry and have a family. Teaching and nursing were seen as 'good professions'. My father was a farmer and women just didn't take over the farm. Not then, anyway.

Today, among the female friends of my generation, I am one of the few who has run a company. Few work. In their social contract they simply weren't expected to. The rules have changed enormously and opportunities for women are far greater, as my friends' daughters are proving. But there's still a long way to go.

Only 3 per cent of people who sit on public boards in Australia are women. And that's just one example.

But I don't see the cause in the same light as many people. It's not that the opportunity isn't there; it's that women have made other choices. Rather than blaming men, look at women who have left the workforce, had families, taken other choices. Because the more realistically that's addressed, the quicker women will move on. In my own life I know that when I've blamed others I haven't progressed a jot.

What's needed is a shift in thinking and although women have made a lot of progress in the workforce, I suspect it may take many years to get long-term change about the way people think.

The rules that haven't changed are those about what works and what doesn't, and for more women to succeed this must be better understood.

Thinking like men

I have a simple formula for female success in business:

> Act like a woman,
> Think like a man,
> Work like a dog

To act like a woman means using female strengths: organisational skills, planning ahead, attention to detail, a tendency to check facts, strong communication skills. And many women would believe they are better than most men at these things. It also means you don't have to disavow your sexuality. I enjoy being feminine, wearing beautiful clothes, meeting men. If I had to compromise my femininity to succeed I wouldn't be prepared to do it because I love being a woman, love everything about the feminine part of my nature. Yet some women try to act like men in business: they want to be aggressive, tough and masculine. That's not the issue.

Thinking like a man is the key. Using the skills

men have developed and putting them into place: taking risks, being tough-minded about decisions, separating emotional and business lives, not fearing independence, trusting their own judgments, genuinely supporting each other.

Many women I see in business confuse the two — they act like men but don't think like men and often these women have lonely jobs that are badly paid. Perhaps that makes them more aggressive. Women who retain their femininity can be very successful because there are a lot of advantages being a woman in business, as long as you can think more like a man does in business.

'Work like a dog' doesn't have an attractive ring to it. In fact many women I've met find that 'work' doesn't have an attractive ring to it! They'd rather be sunbathing or shopping. But a simple truth in the formula for success is hard (smart) work and there's no way around that. It's just that if you're a woman in business it's a bit smarter to sometimes think like a man.

16
LESSONS IN LEADERSHIP

Leadership is leadership of yourself
written in my diary

If business was just about selling or distributing a product it would be easy. It's not.

Business is about people and the relationships you create — relationships with your customers, your suppliers and those you work with. People will either cooperate with you or make your life difficult, depending on how you relate to them. And for the leader of any organisation, successful people relations are fundamental.

As far as I can see the ideal employee is one with ideas who thinks, acts and gets results. Most people have these abilities. It comes down to whether they use them — or whether they can be encouraged to think, act and get results.

In direct-selling organisations such as Pola,

motivation is essential. Without it business goes backwards. And it seems to me that even in a 'normal' job, inspiration and motivation can be a benefit.

Few people can define the term 'motivation'. But once you understand it, it simplifies many things. It is simply this:

> A motive is the inner urge that moves a person.
> So good motivation,
> is the action
> taken to satisfy the inner urge.

To be motivated daily you need to know what your motives are, the plan of action, the goals. This applies to leaders equally as to those under their leadership.

Many companies have mission statements. Many are a bit glib. Some seem to be written because they look good on a business card. The aims of the company, its goals, its mission, must be clear to all. If you have a mission statement, the questions are: Does your team know? Do they share your vision?

If a goal is only your's you're not going to excite other people about it. And they have to share in the rewards if they are to contribute. Sometimes this is financial, and employees owning shares in a company or being in a profit-share deal can be a great way to focus people towards the same goals. If people know you have their best interests at heart, along with the interests of the business, you'll be able to work through obstacles and areas of conflict with them. But if the interests of the individual and the interests of the organisation are out of sync, then there has to be a separation. And the people leave.

In running Pola, with its thousands of consultants over the years, I've noticed that when the values of the organisation are no longer held by the individuals, the individuals invariably leave. And it's better they leave sooner rather than later because it's just too stressful for everyone involved.

People won't follow you if they don't share your vision. And there's no point forcing people to toe the line. In the military they may say 'Jump!' and you say 'How high?' And it works. But the object of the military in war is to defend and destroy. In business it is to build.

Of course, leaders must first learn to follow. I did so with Lionel Ward and the Wool Corporation and later with John Taylor.

If you have complete faith in what you are doing then you have the ability to take others with you. You have to lead by example.

My motivation has been the possibility of achieving success and remaining excited about what I do. Results are more important than recognition. And this relates, in turn, to financial and emotional rewards.

What was often a challenge at Pola was to find what motivated individuals, because the motivations were as different as the people themselves! Most, however, were motivated by the following:

Praise and recognition

Most individuals need motivation and encouragement, and many companies just don't give it to them, which I find amazing. Some only offer a pat on the back when the annual sales and performance review comes around.

But it's so easy to give people simple praise when it's due: 'You did a great job' or 'It's great working with you.' It's only a little thing but it can produce big results.

Competition

In a business where sales figures were important, some were motivated by beating other people. I ensured the figures were published in the monthly magazine along with photos of the top achievers.

Incentives

Cash and travel were big lures in Pola. On one occasion it backfired for the company when one winner went to Japan and hated it, devastated by the tiny size of the rooms we stayed in. For many, though, travel was an irresistible opportunity for adventure. A lot of the women who went on overseas Pola trips had never been outside Australia before. Your first international hotel experience stays with you.

Fear

Several of the top achievers were motivated by fear of not having money or success. It drove them to achieve better and better results.

Belonging

Many direct-selling companies have their origins in Baptist and Mormon churches in the United States and people have traditionally joined to belong to a group they feel comfortable with. While Pola had no such links, quite a few people joined and stayed because of the perceived security the company provided.

Goal-setting

Some people used Pola as a method to build their goal-setting skills by setting and meeting sales targets, while at the same time making money.

Self-improvement

Some joined the company as an opportunity for personal growth. I saw part of my role as leader to encourage women to develop their independence and personal responsibility, an aspect of which was to organise seminars and provide motivational material. Some women attended every seminar and read every piece of literature with the aim of becoming successful, but they never actually did anything!

Money

This was the prime motive.

Some women wanted to make lots of money, others simply to support themselves or their children. It is the main reason why most people join direct-selling companies and no doubt a big motivating force in most industries. At Pola the link between sales and income was generous and direct. One single mother joined with the sole aim of making money and gaining financial security, and had, within three years, bought a house and furnished it, bought a car and put her child into a private school. She then began saving to buy a holiday house.

My role at Pola was both as leader and manager. I had to look at the compass — the big picture, the direction — and the clock — the day-to-day systems and activities of the company. I made many mistakes in both roles, ranging from misjudging people to choosing useless computer systems. But I also learned many aspects of what produced successful leadership.

I learned discipline was essential: I had to put *musts* before *wants*. I had to communicate clearly with people and tell them what I expected of them. And I always made sure they understood. I ensured people knew what the company goals were, so we worked as a team, all moving in the same direction. I was always enthusiastic, because I discovered that enthusiasm boomeranged — if you gave it, it came back. People I valued I respected. And that made for a good work environment. I encouraged people to succeed in their goals — the more successful people are around you, the happier you can be as a leader. At the same time I kept my distance personally, not mixing business and emotional aspects of life.

I had to learn patience with people, especially when they made mistakes. I had to forget losses and tell people not to dwell on a mistake, but to learn from it and move on. And not repeat it. It seemed to me that so few people were prepared to take responsibility for themselves — most believed someone else should be keeping them — and actually go out and work hard.

A key to getting the most from your people is to build the concept of personal responsibility. I heard a variation of this lament many times:

> I work as hard as anyone
> And yet I get so little done.
> I'd do so much, you'd be surprised,
> If I could just get organised.

For a long time I resisted delegating, but I learned that only through empowering others in business can you succeed. They had to take responsibility, make mistakes and learn. I had to remind myself that I'd made many, many mistakes and needed plenty of advice. And as leader, I had to be patient.

I learned not to accept excuses and at the same time not lay blame on people. I found it more productive to address a mistake as a system problem and ask why the mistake happened, not in terms of the person's failing but the system's failing.

An example: if someone left a telephone message and it failed to reach me, it wasn't the fault of the person who took the message. It was the system. We had to find a way where the system wouldn't let it happen again by, say, instituting a telephone message book and initialling the message. That way the person didn't feel rebuked and resentful, but knew enough not to make the same error again. And their ideas in finding a solution that improved the system gave them a sense of ownership and responsibility.

17
SELLING SECRETS

Selling = Relating
John Taylor

When I joined Pola the hardest part was the selling. It took me weeks to summon up the courage to make my first presentation. I had the idea that selling was about pushy, insincere people with dollar signs on their minds. This might have been acceptable if I was dealing with strangers, but I was selling Pola products to friends. I was very hesitant about recommending and imposing my views on people.

I think this came from my academic background: I thought there was something shoddy or sleazy about being in sales. Today, such an idea seems stupid, naive and unreal.

I asked John Taylor to define selling for me and he gave me a definition that not only changed my attitude but my life. It gave me the drive to go out and sell. His definition is still the most embracing I have heard:

Selling = Relating

So if selling is relating — and I believe it is — it seems the most instructive way to look at the art of selling is to look at the art of relating.

Selling is a negotiation, an opportunity for me to persuade people I've got something worth their while participating in. It is an art form that is a sophisticated, exciting way to earn a living and applies to so much about what we do and who we are. We are selling all the time as we relate to others.

These are the keys to relating (selling).

Self-belief

You might try a product and really believe it feels great, but that's different to believing in yourself. Success begins with your self-belief because from that you are able to sell ideas to other people. People rarely buy ideas from people they don't trust or believe in, and if you don't trust or believe in yourself there's only a very small chance of convincing anyone about who you are and what you're doing. The biggest struggle I had initially was believing in myself because my marriage was over, I was broke and I didn't really feel great about myself. If you are low on self-belief others will not find you very convincing.

Belief in your product

If you believe in the integrity of your product, your ability to service that product, its value for money and its benefit to your client, it doesn't matter whether you're selling tyres or tickets or T-bones. If you don't believe in your product, stop selling it now. If it's not going to benefit your client, you are not going to be able to build a business. You will only damage your credibility and, more important, your view of yourself. And I think it is especially important for women to believe in their product. It might seem a sweet, naive way of doing business but it is one that works in the end. Integrity is all-important.

Before I came across Pola I worked for three months as a marketing consultant for a friend who'd bought into a 'revolutionary new product' called PowerSaver. The technology had been developed by NASA and he'd bought 3000 black boxes that would shut off the electricity supply to big pieces of machinery such as lifts when they were not in use, thus saving thousands of dollars in power.

The trouble was it didn't work — one test we did even increased the amount of power being used. I tried in vain to convince people to try one of the black boxes, but once I discovered the product didn't work, I couldn't go on. It became a matter of finding the best way to get out of the deal, but for my (male, actually) friend there was no way out. He lost an enormous amount of money.

Unfortunately, a lot of the salespeople I've seen in action have only really reinforced a negative point of view. People I've encountered in real estate particularly, had a sales patter that was completely dishonest. Best location, most wonderful house in the street and so on . . . You just wonder how people can say these things when they must know it's not true. They must think people who believe these stories are stupid, because no other explanation holds up.

You can con some of the people some of the time, but you can't convince all the people all of the time about something that isn't true or doesn't work. And I would just hate to go to work with that sort of struggle on my hands. How am I going to con another lot of people? The struggle for those people to live a life without integrity must be awfully draining.

Interest in Others

The start of a great relationship is being interested in the other person. Likewise, this is where a great sale starts. Great salespeople don't have to be great talkers but they do have to be great listeners, because the more they know about their prospective customer the more they can sell. If they don't enjoy people they will probably find it hard to make friends and hard to make sales. I always said to potential Pola recruits, If you don't like people, please don't join Pola. Go somewhere else, because it is a criteria that is fundamental to direct selling. Just about every business is dependent on relationships with people. Only the degree varies.

Being Positive

This does not mean a forced cheerfulness that is worn on the sleeve only as long as required. People cannot be fooled so easily, and this type of behavior is off-putting and makes people wary: 'What is she selling now?' Positivity is much deeper than this. It is a way of looking at the world that enables us to retain our sense of humor and perspective. It is a way of looking for the best in people and letting them see that same trait in us.

Enthusiasm

Enthusiasm is different from being positive. It is essentially the way we express our positivity, the ability to communicate our positivity, the quality that lights up a room, makes people walk towards us and not away. Enthusiasm about life and people is more important than enthusiasm about a product. Genuine enthusiasm is not gushy, which pushes people away, it is a magnet that attracts. Selling must be very stressful if you have to feign enthusiasm about a product or you are down on the world. Enthusiasm that is genuine is a delightful quality that lends itself to building relationships — and sales.

Presentation

Much is written about details of presentation, but little about its totality. This is not just the color and shape of your suit but the look in your eyes, the smile on your face, an appearance that reflects warmth and interest. Presentation is about stature, how you hold yourself with genuine pride in yourself, but it is also about warmth and openness to others. It is about dignity and is very powerful. Your total package is how you are judged and related to by others. Note that people sometimes buy from you to be more like you.

Product benefit

Customers do not buy a product, they buy the benefit of the product — for them. That's why it is so important to know what your customer can gain from acquiring your product. People want benefits or advantages that will satisfy their drives and desires, which can be varied. From my experience, people want, in varying order, differing from person to person, changing their wants over time, the following:

- Comfort
- To look better
- To feel better
- To save money
- To make money
- To have romance
- The love of family
- To protect loved ones
- To satisfy curiosity
- Pleasure or amusement
- To gain more leisure time
- To be like others

- To be different from others
- To have variety
- To have security
- To have adventure
- To satisfy the desire to create
- To free themselves from the fear of loss
- Safety
- To obtain recognition
- To win social approval

People have needs and wants: needs are logical, wants are often emotional. As a salesperson, the key is to identify the unique selling propositions of your product and relate these to the customer's particular desire.

The sale

The same process that occurs in building a relationship occurs in a sale. Getting attention, getting interest, creating desire, conviction, then action. So once you are convinced about the value of your product to the customer, be sure you make the sale! It sounds obvious but sometimes we have so much fun relating to people we forget the purpose. As *The One Minute Salesperson* says, 'The purpose of the sale is to give someone else what they want so you get what you want.'

Dealing with rejection

When I had my shop in Armadale, one of the things I thought were so special and amazing was a line of beautiful Valentino screens, but they sat there, ignored.

We had to reduce them down, down, down in price and in the end it was any price just to get rid of them. That was one of the things in the shop that I loved most but it was the thing that wasn't taken up by the clients.

Just as in relationships, at times we have to deal with rejection, and for some people this is hard to take. If you can't handle the fact that not everyone will like you, not everyone will buy from you, then you'll find it very tough in sales. And it is important to accept rejection gracefully. It is just business. It's very important that you give people the opportunity to make their own decision about a purchase because so often the products you have extraordinary faith in, others don't see the value of. This is a matter of integrity, of not imposing your values on others.

Direct Selling

Direct selling in its purest form and following its purest intention is very win-win. You join an organisation and learn about the product, the system of marketing and in turn you teach other people that system, in fact you duplicate yourself — and that's the core concept of direct selling.

Direct selling does offer some guarantees because there is in most cases already a system that is going, the company holds the stock, you don't have to employ people, the financial outlay is minimal — the only risk is you may not succeed at it.

Yet a lot of the people who join these companies are only interested in their own immediate gain, so they'll say anything to people, they'll con them into believing anything, which is a stupid business principle. It is short-lived. That sale alienates potential customers for years to come. It also means the industry has, in many areas, a very poor reputation and one of the great battles I had in building Pola was to try and convince people that the company was credible, that what I said about incomes was credible, because often people had been conned before in the direct selling industry.

People who say that if you join XYZ company you are going to make half a million dollars in year one, talk nonsense. And you don't just make money by recruiting other people. Recruiting is only one means by which you make money in a direct selling company — by that I mean recruiting your sales team. You have to build customers, because it doesn't matter how many people are in your sales team, if none of them is selling anything then you don't have a business. It all comes back to your relationship with your customers and that comes back to your belief in your company, your product and yourself. And success in business begins with your self-belief because from that you are able to sell ideas to other people.

18

JAPANESE

Contributing to the prosperity of a bountiful and peaceful society and the advancement of culture through the business of beauty and health

corporate philosophy, Pola Japan

Pola Inc. has an annual turnover of about $US3 billion. Its products are overwhelmingly directed towards women: cosmetics, jewellery, lingerie. Yet, as far as I know, in the 15 years I was associated with the company, there were no women above junior management level. Then there was me, by default, a Caucasian woman heading up two countries' operations.

I never had any illusion that I would have a more global role in the company. This was the place for Japanese men. And I was aware that my position was due to the success I had in building the business.

My relationship with Pola Japan gave me some tremendous insights into the workings of a big Japanese company, and the context of this chapter is based on what I came across. I don't pretend what I saw was typical of all Japanese business, but as that country slides deeper into recession with an apparent lack of energy, direction and decisiveness by the political leadership, it seems to reflect some of what I saw at Pola.

As much as we don't understand the Japanese they simply don't understand us, nor do they have any great desire to understand us. I didn't mind this attitude because no one had to pretend anything. All we had to do was get on with business.

I hardly learned any of the language, partly because I was too busy to do so in the early years of Pola, and because I feel it's a language that if you don't speak well it's better not to speak it at all. Despite visiting Japan 27 times, and meeting the same people on many occasions, I feel I have got no closer to them, with perhaps one exception — and that relationship is based more on business respect than anything else.

Chauvinism

The arrogance of some men at Pola was the sort that would drive even the mildest feminist crazy. One lunchtime in Tokyo I sat down with some of the young girls in Pola who told me they found it very difficult working with Japanese men. The men considered them not serious about their job and treated them as inferior. Most wanted to leave because of this behavior. I noticed over the years that most young women stayed only a short period of time; they either married, had children or left. It was a short working life.

These young women couldn't believe the sort of life that I lived in Australia. The ability to make my own decisions, live my own life, make my own income, travel round the world, do the things I wanted to do. That concept was difficult for them to understand because they didn't feel they could rise to any level of seniority.

There were exceptions to this rule, men with more sophisticated views of women's roles, but they were far outnumbered and outpowered in the company. And they certainly weren't those who made the decisions.

Decision-making

One of the most frustrating aspects was decision-making. It appears individuals were not empowered to make individual decisions and, as I got to better understand the system, I realised the process was designed more for self-protection than for good outcomes. For even the smallest idea to be accepted there was a process that slowed business and caused enormous frustration. The fear of making a bad decision was more important than the possibility of taking a successful risk.

When Pola tried to break into the US retail market it lost millions, as it had done in other countries. Yet the worst that seemed to happen to these decision-makers was that they were moved to other parts of the company and were often replaced by people who were less competent. No women were promoted.

As a business principle, the combination of a number of brains outweighs the value of one brain. Effective decision-making is a combination of ideas and the leadership necessary to ensure action. But when a company is bogged down with old ideas and a fear of taking risks, the business is certain to stall in today's competitive, constantly changing world.

The seniority system made this worse. The road is long and hard for individuals in corporate Japan: years of service are highly regarded and give someone more pull than creativity or individual talent. So those with little talent but a long service record could have great influence, over and above a talented, dynamic staff member with fewer years' service.

Meetings

The first time the Japanese came to Australia we met in a hotel room, literally all day, to discuss a very small number of matters, tiny matters that really could have been resolved very quickly. At the end of a couple of hours we had to start the discussion all over again when we realised that no one had understood a word of what we were saying. And yet no one could admit to not understanding. We had to find ways to determine whether there really was agreement, like repeating back and getting them to repeat back what we'd said. It was slow and frustrating.

And generally, having got to the end of a long discussion about a fairly small issue, they would say, 'We'll have to take it [somewhere else] and let you know the outcome at a later date.'

On my visits to Japan the pattern was the same. Because of the fear of individuals making mistakes, even the smallest decision required a meeting. And for hours we would discuss trivia while my key concerns — especially product price and marketing support — would not be addressed. We all know the jokes about committees and their inherent problems. Some of these meetings turned those jokes into an art form.

Politeness

The Japanese culture has many enviable aspects, not least of which is the politeness and charm of many of the customs. I appreciated the many small distinctions of politeness, such as gift-giving and controlled behavior in business situations. But I also learned that behind this external charm, the politics were cut-throat. Some individuals would say things to me about each other that I found extraordinary. I don't believe people from, say, an American company, would come to Australia and say: 'I hate that person.' Yet they could say on one hand they hated each other, but they'd be totally civilised and polite towards each other. Maybe that veneer of politeness in Japanese society means frictions between people become very pent-up.

Social behavior

At the end of a frustrating day-long meeting I would often be stressed. The last thing I could imagine myself enjoying would be spending time with the same people I'd been having a tough day with. But in Japanese thinking, 'Well, it's 6 o'clock, so that's over, and now let's go to a karaoke bar, have a lot to drink and really relax.'

And on these sometimes drunken evenings more truth would be revealed than during a whole day of meetings. People would sing, lurch about and get drunk.

Yet the next day we had to forget that we ever had

that evening out. I soon learned it was poor form to ever raise the issue of anything that occurred the night before. The most one would say would be: 'Thank you very much for a very pleasant dinner last night.' And that would be it. There would be no further discussion about what happened, who chose what song, who sang off-key, who drank too much. I found it baffling that such a distinction could be made between business and social outings and concluded that these evenings were stress breakers that reflect the truly stressful lives Japanese live.

Another area that intrigued me was the way partners did not become involved in business life. At first it was a bit disconcerting, as in Western organisations partners play key roles in entertaining and organising. But I realised it could be helpful. Partners can be interfering, often don't really know what they are talking about, and have likes and dislikes about the people you work with that can add another layer of possible problems.

I never met the wives of any of the men I worked with. The closest I got was vaguely hearing whether they had a wife or children. And I found it fascinating that in a direct-selling organisation, where personal contact is very much the key, even the wife of the president never appeared at any of the annual conventions, where 3000 of the top people in Pola gathered. In Japanese eyes apparently, if you're not in the company you're not in the company.

Friendship

The most interesting aspect of my involvement with Pola was the separation of business and friendships. At other places I've worked, co-workers often become friends. At Pola Japan it was different.

It was like doing business in a personal vacuum, which had many disadvantages because it was hard to work out what anyone was thinking or why. But the advantages were that I didn't get bogged down or involved in people's personal lives. Conversation about personal lives was limited to the nights at dinner or in bars, and even then I didn't really get a picture of how someone really thought.

The only insight I've had that was really quite fascinating for me was a woman in the company who I'll call Yoko. We'd been to dinner many times but I still felt pretty remote from her. Then one day I got an extraordinary fax.

She said she was finally leaving Pola. She'd told me once she had a boyfriend and I got the impression without her ever really saying this that he was the love of her life. The fax said how much she'd enjoyed working with me, how much she liked me, and that she had now caught up with her college boyfriend and was leaving the company and going to Paris to live. It was a really warm and loving letter that ended with hearts and kisses. It was really affectionate and I was intrigued. Our association had been strictly businesslike and there had been none of this apparent warmth or real feeling. I sent a fax back saying she'd been really great to work with and I wished her all the best and great happiness in Paris and thought, that's that.

I went to Japan about six months later and I was stunned to see Yoko back in the company. She was in the same department but had no contact with Australia. I spent about four days there. She smiled at me. I smiled back. A glass wall had gone up again and we couldn't recover the personal part. And in the end my curiosity completely overcame me and I said to her: 'I'm so surprised to see you back in Pola because I had a lovely letter from you and you said you were going to Paris. What happened?'

She just looked at me and a single tear started to well in the corner of her eye. She simply stared at me as the tear ran slowly down her face. I think there was more emotion in that single tear than in any of the tears I've seen before or since. I got a life story of disappointment, the break-up of the relationship, the loss of face coming back to the same company — everything showed on her face with that single tear. And yet she didn't waver in looking at me. Even though I went on to work with Yoko again, it was the last time the subject was ever raised or discussed.

Budgets and figures

The Japanese are well known for their attention to detail, particularly in the area of budgets and figures. I learned to become very conscious of the figures of business and that one should estimate future profits conservatively. This happened in my first year at Pola when I set a target for the budget, which I considered a goal. I didn't meet it but was pleased I'd got close and business had grown. The Japanese were appalled. In their eyes I'd failed, because I hadn't met my budget, so I lost my bonus. I realised then that it was a communication problem.

Head office was always keen to know statistics and figures, and communication was frequent. But sometimes I received faxes from Japan that were so aggressive and offensive they made me want to turn my back on the company. A junior clerk would sign a note saying: 'We demand to know the exact reasons for poor sales in Sydney.' I'd be stunned. But when I thought about it, the choice of words was usually the problem: they were asking why Sydney's sales for the month had fallen slightly.

Yet in consistency and quality control, Pola was extraordinary. Each month for 15 years a shipment of goods was delivered from Japan and only once, in only one box, was the content not what it should have been. I wish we'd made as few mistakes sending out orders to our consultants over the same time.

In all my negotiations about money, Pola Japan staff paid a great deal of attention to the numbers. When I left the company, each dollar I was owed in holiday pay, superannuation and the like was accounted for, to the cent.

I learned to love Japan, Japanese civility and the country's charming customs. I also learned a great deal about the business culture and practices that have helped Japan to become the world's second biggest economy. While I believe the Japanese business system has some weaknesses, there many lessons we can adopt and use in Australia.

19
MANAGING MONEY

Money is like a sixth sense without which you cannot make a complete use of the other five

W Somerset Maugham

In the 1970s money was no problem.

My husband and I at various stages owned houses, a farm, a property on the beach. We lived well: holidays, restaurants, parties, the races, expensive cars.

Money was no problem because I knew nothing about it.

Growing up in the country I'd learned conservative values about money and in my overseas travels I'd been good at making it last. But that was the limit of my experience. My friends and I never discussed money, taxation, negative gearing, investments, shares or superannuation. Money was left to the men.

As a result of this stupidity I paid the price, left broke when my marriage ended in the early 1980s. Almost all the wealth we lost was because of crazy schemes to minimise tax that lost far more than they ever saved. In retrospect, unsophisticated as it was, country conservatism and a careful traveller's purse management was a sounder basis for money management than the overly clever 1980s-style schemes.

I had committed what I now realise was a cardinal sin. I had not taken responsibility. It was such a waste and a rather sad reckoning after 11 years of marriage.

As a result money became something of a demon for me and I set myself two missions. First, to become financially independent, and second to teach as many women as possible about taking responsibility for money.

Had I not become broke I doubt I would have learned as much as I have about money. For five years I curbed my spending and lived frugally. I still have a lot to learn and I continually seek advice from accountants, successful friends and finance professionals about money management. Now, among my friends, money, taxation, negative gearing, investments, shares and superannuation are all topics that come up in discussion among the anecdotes, gossip and jokes. For women, money, an irrelevant subject in the 1960s and 1970s, is fundamental to living in the 1990s.

Understanding money simply makes life freer and easier. Its mismanagement causes undue stress.

There are some simple rules about money which I wish I'd known about when I started work at 21!

It is important to treat money with respect as it is hard to earn and can be a source of great satisfaction if used wisely.

When you know what you want — whether it's a

house, a car, a pair of shoes or even paying off the credit card — there are four fundamental rules: set earnings goals, set savings goals, budget with care, and borrow only under certain circumstances.

Earnings goals

If you have your own business, you may think it's impossible to set earnings goals but I believe it is possible to work out your income and set realistic goals. If you are on a salary it is much easier. The key is to be realistic and set time frames.

Savings goals

It's certainly possible to set savings goals, which again must be realistic. Some contingency fund for emergencies is advisable. A savings goal is contingent on covering the necessities, which, of course, is a personal matter. What you consider necessary others might see as a luxury. It very much depends on how serious you are about saving money.

Budgeting

Everyone needs a budget because without one, rich people can become poor quickly. And poor people poorer.

Having set earnings and savings goals, the money you have left forms your spending budget. What you spend it on is mostly clear: food, rent or mortgage, clothes, petrol etc. The fundamental thing is once you've worked out how best to spend this money, you *stick to the budget.*

I have found that if a savings goal is sufficiently attractive, sticking to the budget is made a lot easier.

In buying my house I set a budget for every dollar I spent. It was amazing to discover what my money went on and how my hard-earned dollars had been disappearing. My strategy was to decide exactly what I was prepared to do without — and then stick to it until I paid for my house.

I set a time frame that, while a fair way away, was close enough to see. And then it was a matter of discipline. Each time I sacrificed something I could see the reward. And when I finally paid off my mortgage there was a huge sense of relief and achievement. I celebrated with French champagne — and began setting new financial goals.

Borrowing

Simple. Only borrow for assets or cash flow. Never borrow for luxuries.

Borrow for a mortgage because a house is an asset that, if all things are equal, can be sold again at a reasonable price. Borrow for cash flow if it is for your business — if you need to buy stock that you will sell at a profit, then do so. But don't borrow money to buy a new pair of shoes because you like them, or a new suit. Credit cards are one of the banes of Western society and have financially trapped many people. It's so easy to hand over a piece of plastic for an impulse purchase. If you force yourself to go to a bank, withdraw the cash, go back to the seller and hand the money over, you will have better understood whether you really need to make the purchase.

Many people spend their lives earning a living rather than designing their lives. Imagine spending 40 years doing something that you dislike so that you can retire. Studies show most people work at things they are unhappy with. What a waste of a life. It seems to me that each year has to be lived to the fullest, which means it is critical that when we do earn money, we enjoy it.

Finally, some simple tips about money:

- Prioritise your spending
- Buy quality
- Enjoy what you spend on
- Don't be influenced by what others have
- Save a percentage of what you earn each week
- Celebrate the achievement of financial goals
- Never borrow for luxuries
- Achieve your needs first, then spend on your wants

20
CHANGE

The only certainty in life (aside from death and taxes) is change. Embrace it.

written in my diary

After 15 years with Pola I decided the fun and the challenge had gone. I had spent longer in Pola than in my marriage and had certainly put more time into Pola than any other aspect of my life.

I sub-consciously began preparing for change — a sort of self-protection mechanism — when I was in New York in January 1996. The book of the moment was Michael Gelb's *Thinking for a Change* and I bought it and read it on the plane back to Australia. It was the start of my own decision to prepare for personal change.

When I began to raise and support Pola's profile, I accepted almost all invitations (generally 7am breakfast talks — sometimes as many as four a week) to address business conventions, sales meetings, business clubs and women's groups, I hadn't bargained on the snowball effect it would have. In addition to being a very direct and effective way of attracting clients and consultants to Pola I also got enormous pleasure from the responses I got.

When Barry Markoff invited me to become a client of International Celebrity Management I could see the opportunity of this skill in any business beyond Pola.

I had always known Pola Australia was vulnerable to someone from Pola's International Department deciding they would like to control the business, a Japanese man running the office in Australia. I had this feeling because there were a number of men in that department who'd indicated the fact to me — the hints were subtle, but there nonetheless. Unfortunately these were some of the least competent men I'd met at Pola.

I knew that if these people became involved I would not want to stay. Although my relations with Pola over the years had been excellent, few of these particular men were people I respected. It was those men who had been largely involved in unsuccessful aspects of Pola's international business.

In August 1997 I realised my concerns were about to happen — head office was set to interfere in areas foreign to them and I felt this would damage the business.

I also knew Pola was no longer interested in expanding further into Caucasian markets, which for some time they had been keen to do, especially in the United States — the business there had ended up making sales almost exclusively to Korean and Hispanic Americans. I had been keen to expand from Australia into the US, targetting its massive Caucasian market. I was certain Pola Australia could recruit there using the system I'd established. I'd already proved that it could be transferred from country to country by moving into New Zealand. But the men running the International Department were not interested. The corporate politics were not on my side. And I was a woman — I'd experienced a fair share of resentment for holding the position I did. And, more importantly, I was not Japanese.

All in all, it was time to move on — but making the break was extremely difficult.

I really loved so many aspects of the business: the products, the people, the direct-selling industry. I enjoyed being chief executive officer, the variety it offered, the opportunity to develop new skills in so many areas from video production to public speaking to balance-sheet analysis.

I felt comfortable in the space I had created in the business. It was like my home. I'd had the time and opportunity to create a physical environment which reflected the tone of the business — a harmony between the Japanese culture and the feel of a cosmetic company in Australia.

There is no doubt that all change is difficult and the longer we remain somewhere the harder it is to change.

I also had to deal with self-belief — would I be able to create or develop another business? I had become so identified with Pola both in my own mind and in the eyes of my consultants and customers that I felt leaving would be disloyal.

Years earlier I had engaged a public relations firm to look at raising the profile of the company. Their suggestion had been that the only ongoing publicity that Pola could expect without spending a fortune would be to tell my story and in doing so become a role model for other women.

My first reaction was negative. I had, then, no desire to tell my story for the sake of the business. But I realised that advertising was not possible for the product because there was simply not that sort of money — so free publicity was the only way to spread the Pola story. It was at this point that my identity and that of Pola became entwined, which made my decision to leave harder.

My last day at Pola, 24 December 1997, was indeed a very emotional one and I spent most of the day hiding tears — a very strange way to voluntarily leave an organisation. I was aware that the gap in my life by leaving Pola would be great but I simply had to keep telling myself, 'No pain, no gain.'

I decided that one of the ways I would be able to deal with the change would be to travel for a month in order to have a break from the routine I'd become so used to. The day I returned to Melbourne was very hard. Normally I would go home, shower and go straight to the office, but that day there was no office to go to. Worse, there was no personal assistant to send faxes, letters and supply me with details on what had been happening in my absence. I felt truly desolate and cut off from the world.

It made me realise what a critical role family and friends play in our lives.

Within days I'd bought a printer for my home computer and a fax and set up a home office. And I quickly discovered the disciplines needed there: set working times, set break times and a clearly designated work area, for starters. I consulted successful workers from home and listed their tips.

And I embraced change and the release and challenge of change because, like death and taxes, it is the only certainty in life.

The pro-active role I'd had at Pola began to work for me. The challenge? What I had taught people for years I now had an opportunity to apply to myself. I was now in a new business, the business of re-engineering my life, finding a new dream, making my plans and taking action.

I'm sure to make many mistakes on this new path. It's inevitable. In this book I've covered some of the worst I've made so far and I'm well aware that at times I've been pathetically passive, naive and out-of-touch, just to name a few sins. At the front of my diary in 1987, the year I became CEO of Pola, I wrote a saying that suggests fears of poor performance were strong in my mind that year. I wrote: 'Anything worth doing is worth doing badly at first' and I think that is a realistic, optimistic and positive way of taking new steps, facing change and handling such fears.

Over the past 15 years I've asked thousands of women the three questions that follow. Their answers determined the paths they took, just as my answers 15 years ago determined mine. Now I'm asking myself the same questions anew. The answers will still be my own, no one else's, and they will be today's answers, because now is the only time that counts. And they'll determine the quality of my life in the next century.

Equally, the quality of your answers will determine the quality of your life. Good luck.

   What is it you want?
   What are you willing to do to get what you want?
   When are you willing to start to get what you want?

RECOMMENDED READING

Go For It	Dr Irene Kassorla
The One Minute Manager	Kenneth Blanchard, Spencer Johnson
The One Minute Salesperson	Spencer Johnson, Larry Wilson
If You Want To Be Rich and Happy, Don't Go to School	Robert Kiyosaki
How to Master the Art of Selling	Tom Hopkins
Awaken the Giant Within	Anthony Robbins
Leadership is an Art	Max De Pree
Leadership Jazz	Max De Pree
The Seven Habits of Highly Effective People	Stephen Covey

First Things First	Stephen Covey, A Roger Miller
Thinking for a Change	Michael J Gelb
The E Myth Revisited	Michael Gerber
The Secrets of the Rain Maker	Chin Ning Chu
Passionate People Produce	Charles Kovess
The Seven Spiritual Laws of Success	Deepak Chopra
The Road Less Travelled	M Scott Peck
The Road From Coorain	Jill Ker Conway
The Magic of Conflict	Tom Crum
How Men Think	Adrienne Mendell

CONTACTS

For speaking engagements
Marcia Griffin can be contacted directly
on e-mail
marcia_griffin@msn.com

or

ICM Speakers and Entertainers
(03) 9529 3711
or tollfree 1800 334625
International + 61 + 3 + 9529 3711

or write
International Celebrity Management
187 Greville Street
Prahran 3181
Facsimile (03) 9529 4573

HIGH-HEELED SUCCESS

ACKNOWLEDGEMENTS

My life has been full of people who have supported, challenged and encouraged me to give my best. It is these people I wish to thank. Some I have not named, but you know who you are. Thank you.

First and foremost thanks to Mum and Dad, who continue to inspire me. I love you. To my brothers and sisters for sharing their hopes and dreams. To Neil Griffin for his support in my early adult life. To my friends who have given unending support in the tough times: Lizzie Webb for her countless roast dinners and laughter; Caz Moran for her honesty and concern; Si Bennett for her quiet courage that proves women are really amazing. To soul mates Cevin Larner, Gale Paine, Gloria Krope, Yvonne Rowe, Susie Drever, Danny DeCapelle, Bronnie Neck and Joy Ross. To Pat

Parkinson for sharing travels to remote parts of Asia as a university student. And to Liz Polk, who first taught me some of the secrets of business.

Thanks also to some exceptional men, notably mentor and business guru John Taylor, Bill Pollock, John McMurrick, Charles Kovess, Bruce Lilley, John Forehan, Steve Wood and Clive Benson-Brown. All gave me friendship and helped unravel the mysteries of the male mind. And special thanks to Gregory Landsman, Paul Adorna, Tony Shaw and Hilton Grimmer, and Graeme Alford, who sowed the seed of this book in my mind.

Finally, to the people I worked with at Pola for 15 years; my office team, whose talents were extraordinary; the thousands of consultants who taught me so much about life; and the many people in Japan I met over the years. Thank you all.